Jump into Jazz

Jump into Jazz

A Primer for the
Beginning Jazz Dance Student

Minda Goodman Kraines
Mission College

Esther Kan
Solano Community College

 Mayfield Publishing Company

Library of Congress Catalog Card Number: 82-073739
International Standard Book Number: 0-87484-571-8

Manufactured in the United States of America
Mayfield Publishing Company
1240 Villa Street, Mountain View, CA 94041

Sponsoring editor: C. Lansing Hays
Manuscript editor: Mary Anne Stewart
Managing editor: Pat Herbst
Art director: Nancy Sears
Designer: Brenn Lea Pearson
Illustrator: Mary Burkhardt
Production manager: Cathy Willkie
Compositor: Publisher's Typography
Printer and binder: The Book Press

Contents

Preface   *ix*

1   Jazz Dance: A History   2
Jazz Dance: What Is It?   3
The Beginning   4
Minstrel Shows   4
The 1920s   6
The 1930s   7
The 1940s   9
The 1950s   10
The 1960s   13
The 1970s   15
The 1980s   17

2   Getting Started   18
Attire   20
  Women's Clothing   20
  Men's Clothing   20
  Footwear   20
Appearance   20
Etiquette   21
Basic Structure of a Jazz Dance Lesson   21
  Pre–Warm-up   21
  Warm-up   21
  Isolation Movements   22
  Locomotor Movements   22
  Dance Movements   22

3   A Dancer's Posture   24
Posture and Alignment   26
Alignment Reference Points   27
Placement   27
  The Pelvis   28
  The Rib Cage   28
  The Shoulder Girdle   28
  The Head and Neck   29
  The Feet   29
  The Knees   29
Alignment Exercises   30

4   Ballet for the Jazz Dancer   34
Turnout   36
Positions of the Feet   36
Positions of the Arms   37
  First Position   37
  Second Position   37
  Third Position   37
  Fourth Position   37
  Fifth Position   38
Ballet Movements   38
  Plié   39
  Relevé   40
  Battements   40
  Arabesque   41
  Attitude   41
  Passé   42

Principles of Movement   42
 Shift of Weight   42
 Jumps   43
 Turns   43

5 Basic Jazz Dance   44

Body Positions   45
 Arch   46
 Contraction   46
 Flat Back   46
 Diagonal Flat Back   47
 Hinge   47
 Jazz Split   47
 Lateral   48
 Lunge   48
Standing Stretches   48
 Lunge with Opposition Stretch   49
 Second Position Parallel Forward Stretch   49
 Second Position Parallel Forward Stretch/
  Bent Knees   49
 Side Stretch   49
 First Position Parallel Forward Stretch   50
 Body Wave or Roll   50
 Back (Released) Stretch   51
 Hand Walk   51
 Runner Lunges   51
Sitting Stretches   52
 First Position Parallel Stretch   52
 Soles-of-the-Feet-Together Stretch   52
 Second Position Straddle Stretch   52
 Jazz Split Stretch   53
 The Plow   54
 The Plow/Straight Legs   54
 The Plow/Pike Stretch   54
 Cobra Stretch/Upper Back Arch   55
Body Isolations   55
 The Head   55
 The Shoulders   56
 The Ribs   56
 The Hips   56

Locomotor Movements   57
 Jazz Walks   57
 Chassé   57
 Pas de Bourrée   57
 Triplet   59
 Jazz Slide   60
 Jazz Square   60
 Hitch Kick   60
 Fan Kick   63
 Kick-Ball Change   64
Oppositional Moves   64
Turns   64
 Paddle Turn   65
 Pivot Turn   65
 Chaîné Turn   65
 Piqué Turn   66
 Pirouette   66
 Soutenu Turn   67
Jumps   67
 Jump   67
 Hop   68
 Assemblé   68
 Sissonne   68
 Leap/Jeté   69

6 Putting It All Together   70

Time: Find the Beat and Count It   72
 Beat   72
 Tempo   72
 Meter and Measure   72
 Time Signature   72
 Note Values   72
 Simple Meter   73
 Compound Meter   73
 Mixed Meter   73
 Accent and Syncopation   73
 Rhythmic Pattern   73
 Musical Phrases   74
 Exercises for the Study of Time   74

Space   75
  Direction   75
  Spatial Pattern   75
  Level   75
  Dimension   76
  Exercises for the Study of Space   76
Dynamics   76
  Exercises for the Study of Dynamics   77
Projection   77
Basic Combinations for Home and Class
  Study   78
    Combination 1   78
    Combination 2   78
    Combination 3   78
    Combination 4   78
    Combination 5   78
    Combination 6   79

7   The Dancer's Instrument: Taking Care of It   80

Pre–Warm-up Exercises   81
  Floor Exercises for the Ankle, Knee, and Hip
    Joints   81
  Standing Exercises for the Upper Torso and
    Weight-bearing Joints   83
Injuries   84
  Muscle Soreness   84
  I-C-E: The Magic Word   84
  Cramp   85
  Strain   85
  Sprain   85
  Shin Splints   85
Nutrition   86
  Protein   86
  Carbohydrates   86
  Fats   86
  Vitamins and Minerals   86
  Calories   87

8   The Dancer's Next Step   88

Additional Training   90
Jazz Dance Styles   90
  Lyrical Jazz   90
  Funky/Disco Jazz   90
  Afro Jazz   90
Jazz Dance Choreography   91
  Music Selection   91
  Music Analysis   91
  Movement Selection   91
  Dance Group Size Selection   91
Jazz Dance Performance   92
  Behind the Performance Scene   92
  Advertisement Design and Distribution   92
  Program Design and Distribution   92
  Sound   93
  Lighting   93
  Costume Design and Wardrobe Assistants   93
  Props and Stagehands   93
  Makeup   93
  Ushering   94
  The Performance Space   94
  The Dance Program   94
  The Performance   94

Addenda

Appendix A. Checklist for a More Successful Dance Class   95

Appendix B. A Future in Jazz Dance   96

Professional Dancer   96
Dance Rehearsal Director   97
Choreographer   98
Dance Teacher   98

Appendix C. Jazz Dance Music 99

Jazz 99
  Metered Jazz 100
  Free-form Jazz 100
  Vocal Jazz 100
  Swing/Big Band/Nostalgia 100
  Ragtime 100
  New Orleans Jazz 100
  Latin Jazz 100
Rock 101
  Soul 101
  Disco 101
  Hard Rock 101

  New Wave 101
  Reggae 101
Blues 101
Vocals 102
Show Tunes 102

Appendix D. Jazz Dance Films 103

Instructional Films 103
Commercial Films 104

Bibliography 107

Index 111

Preface

Increased concern for personal fitness and a growing appreciation of dance have combined to enhance the popularity of jazz dance classes. These classes are now offered at four-year universities, community colleges, adult schools, recreation centers, and health spas.

The appeal of jazz dance stems from its involvement with energy: It is energy in motion, vital and vibrant. Jazz dance movements can be sharp or smooth, quick or slow, exaggerated or subtle. Jazz dance can be expansive leaps or contained turns. Its movements can be performed to a wide range of music, in a variety of moods.

Jazz is an exciting form of dance that can capture your body, heart, and soul. It can create in you a desire to know more about its movements, dynamics, styles, and history.

Although interest and participation in jazz dance have rapidly increased, information regarding the specifics of jazz dance has not been readily available to the novice dancer. *Jump into Jazz* attempts to fill this need by summarizing a substantial body of basic dance techniques and principles, with easy-to-follow examples and illustrations. We hope it will serve as a guide for the beginning student as well as a reference for all those interested in jazz dance.

We begin with a narration of jazz dance's lively history. "Getting Started" then describes appropriate dance attire, class etiquette, and the basic structure of a class. Our introduction to jazz dance continues with chapters on dance posture, ballet for the jazz dancer, and basic jazz dance. The chapter on dance posture defines correct posture and presents a series of easy-to-do posture exercises. The ballet chapter explains basic ballet movements used in the jazz dance class and important ballet techniques. A detailed exposition of a widely accepted jazz dance vocabulary follows, including warm-ups, isolations, and locomotor movements specific to the style of jazz dance.

To help the student put these basics together and dance, the succeeding chapters discuss basic music theory as it applies to dance; the importance of space, dynamics, and projection as a means of creating variety in dance; and several dance combinations for home or classroom study.

Dance is as much a demanding physical activity as it is an art form, and every dancer needs to know the essentials of body maintenance. In "The Dancer's Instrument: Taking Care of It," we therefore discuss preventive methods and first aid for dance injuries, as well as nutritional insights for the dancer. Detailed headings make this chapter a quick and easy reference.

In "The Dancer's Next Step," we provide information on additional training, choreography concepts, and the dance performance onstage and behind the scene. A section on different styles of jazz dance will give the beginning dancer a basic idea of the variety of existing jazz dance forms.

The appendixes, as important as the other chapters, supply a checklist to help ensure the student a more successful dance class, plus an overview of careers available to the jazz dancer. An extensive list of jazz music and jazz dance films is included to enrich the student's experience and provide a source for teaching materials.

For their suggestions and critical reading of an early draft of our manuscript we wish to thank Kay Fulton of Santa Barbara City College, Ann Malmuth-Onn of West Valley College, Dawn S. Sare of Monterey Peninsula College, and Melanie Snyder of California State University at Fresno.

Our hope is that after reading this book, you will surely want to "jump into jazz."

M.G.K.
E.K.

Jump into Jazz

Chapter 1

Jazz Dance:
A History

Louis Armstrong, the famous jazz trumpet player, is quoted as saying, "If you have to ask what jazz is, you'll never know." We do ask the question because we want to know: Jazz dance—What is it? What does it involve? Where did it come from?

JAZZ DANCE: WHAT IS IT?

Jack Cole, a jazz dance innovator, called jazz dance "urban folk dance." Although the primary source of jazz dance is African, its development is a com-

Forty-second Street, *choreographed by Gower Champion in 1980. Photo by Martha Swope.*

bination of African and European influences cultivated in the American urban environment. Jazz dance is a mirror of the social history of the American people, reflecting historical events, cultural changes, ethnic influences, and especially the music and social dances of its eras. It is from this latter perspective that our study of jazz dance history will be viewed.

The essence of jazz dance is its bond to jazz music, and the evolution of jazz dance parallels each developing phase of jazz music. Thus today, jazz dance, like jazz music, comes in many guises—the Broadway show, the concert stage, musical theater, film and television, Las Vegas and Hollywood choruses, and even discotheques.

THE BEGINNING

The origins of jazz music and jazz dance are traced to the rhythms and movements brought to America by African slaves. In Africa, every event of any consequence was celebrated and expressed in music and dance. As arriving slaves, Africans were isolated from their families, their fellow tribesmen, their language, and their tribal traditions. Although slaves were imported from many African cultures, Americans viewed all Africans as from a single culture. As a result, the suppression of individual customs led to an intermingling of African cultures that created a new culture with both African and American elements.

Restrictive slave laws enacted by Southern slave owners prohibited African drums and ritual African dances. However, the prohibition of their native music and dance did not suppress the African slaves' desire to cling to those parts of their cultural identity. The rhythms and movements of African dance endured in foot stamping and tapping, hand clapping, and rhythmic voice sounds.

MINSTREL SHOWS

The rise of the minstrel show in the nineteenth century coincided with a change in the American attitude toward blacks as whites discovered they could identify with certain aspects of the Negro character. The minstrel show was originally initiated by whites in mimicry of blacks; it popularized the African style of dance and music, which depended greatly on solo performance and improvisation. With the Fugitive Act of 1859, many blacks migrated north and replaced the black-faced white minstrel performers.

Although the minstrel show was primarily a Southern art form, its influence affected the whole country with the introduction of the cakewalk. In the original cakewalk, which was performed as a social dance, couples paraded in a circle, creating intricate steps in competition for the prize of a cake—hence the name "cakewalk." Later the cakewalk was performed as the grande finale of the minstrel show. The sense of competition was retained by couples marching elegantly around in a circle, showing off with high kicks and fancy, inventive struts.

With the popularity of minstrel shows and the development of vaudeville, white performers, still in imitation of black dancers, introduced the buck and wing. This dance was strongly influenced by the Irish jig and the English clog, with their fast legwork and footwork and minimal body and arm movement. The buck and wing was a combination of clog, jig, and song and dance and was hallmarked by a syncopated rhythm. It was the dance that introduced the swinging rhythm of jazz, which was not apparent in clogs and jigs. The characteristics of the buck and wing were later incorporated in the graceful and elegant soft shoe, which was originally danced to popular Southern tunes.

With white dancers as the star performers of the

The Joffrey Ballet's interpretation of the cakewalk. Photo by Martha Swope.

minstrel and vaudeville shows, it was difficult for a black dancer to gain stature as part of a troupe. Embittered, many black performers migrated to Europe, where they introduced the newly evolving forms of jazz music and jazz dance. In Europe, these talented and innovative performers were received more readily than in their American homeland. The minstrel show eventually evolved and was absorbed into the twentieth-century musical comedy.

At the close of the minstrel period, the syncopated rhythms of American ragtime bands accompanied the introduction of early forms of jazz dances. The use of syncopation—accenting the offbeat—has been incorporated throughout jazz history and is a trademark of jazz music today. In the brief period of 1910–1915, over a hundred new dances emerged and disappeared from American ballrooms. The most significant of these dances were the fast-paced, hectic, one-step dances. The public outrage caused by these wild dances paved the way for the famous dance team of Vernon and Irene Castle. The Castles brought an elegance to the dances of the period with the refined Castle walk and made dancing a fad in high-society circles. They also popularized a new dance step, the fox trot. Inspired by the musical rhythm style of the blues, the fox trot outlasted all the other dances of the period. At the same time, World War I initiated the novelty of public dancing in restaurants and cabarets, which gave a great impetus to the musical craze called jazz.

THE 1920s

The 1920s marked the end of World War I, and the American public looked forward to a period of prosperity. The dances that emerged during this period reflected the public's need for a sense of gaiety and freedom that was lacking during the war era. Through the end of the 1920s, Dixieland jazz music, with its fast ragtime beat, spread from New Orleans to Chicago and New York. The growth of jazz dance was directly influenced by this musical genre.

For a brief time, exclusively black casts danced to jazz music on the Broadway stage in such musicals as *Shuffle Along* (1921) and *Runnin' Wild* (1923). *Shuffle Along* introduced the dynamic dancer and performer Josephine Baker. Baker was in the chorus line but immediately stood out with mugging and out-of-step movements that were done with such finesse that they became a featured part of the act. She continued to dance on Broadway until she went to Paris, where she became a huge success. Many other black performers also found success in Paris at this time.

Runnin' Wild introduced the Charleston, with dancers using body isolations for the first time in

The wild Charleston set the world dancing in the 1920s. Photo from New York Public Library at Lincoln Center.

social dance. Negro in origin, the Charleston incorporated the fundamentals of hand clapping and foot stamping apparent in the dances of the Old South. The Charleston popularized dancing and stimulated such dances as the big apple and the black bottom, which were performed to dance songs that included dance-step instructions in the lyrics.

This was also the era of Bill "Bojangles" Robinson,

Bill "Bojangles" Robinson, light on his feet and full of charisma. Photo from New York Public Library at Lincoln Center.

a black tap dancer who achieved world fame through the clean and clear percussive rhythms of his feet. The early versions of tap dance evolved from the Irish jig, which incorporated limited upper body movements. As the movements of tap dance became more flexible, the lightness of Robinson's style influenced the future of tap dance by changing the placement of the tap steps from the full foot to the ball of the foot. Bojangles was seen performing on Broadway, in Hollywood films, and in shows that toured the country. His recognition helped to establish the popularity of this dance form.

THE 1930s

The 1920s closed with the introduction of talkies, and the public flocked to the movie houses as the Broadway musical was abandoned. The Depression followed, and people sought an escape from their dreary lives. The 1930s were the era of dance marathons and big bands. Dance competitions became popular, for people were willing to try anything in the hope of winning a cash prize. Jazz music moved away from ragtime, Dixieland, and blues, and a new sound began to emerge with the "symphonic jazz" of Paul Whiteman. Whiteman brought full orchestration to his music and made syncopation a part of every song he played. The substitution of countermelodies for improvisation made his music more danceable.

The black American bands of Duke Ellington and Louis Armstrong also attracted public attention. Their music gave birth to the swing era, which got its start with Duke Ellington's "It Don't Mean a Thing If It Ain't Got Swing." The swing era, also termed the big-band era, was marked by the orchestrated jazz music of such greats as Artie Shaw, Glenn Miller, Benny Goodman, Tommy and Jimmy Dorsey, and Count Basie. Swing music consisted of a simple theme that was improvised on by solo instruments. The dances that evolved during the swing era became an interpretation of the energy that this musical style generates. During this time, the Savoy Ballroom in Harlem, dubbed "The Home of Happy Feet," was the largest ballroom in the world—one square block—and for thirty years, jazz dancers and swing musicians converged here.

The jitterbug at a 1940s dance hall. Improvisation was the key to its excitement. Photo from New York Public Library at Lincoln Center.

The charismatic Fred Astaire, showing nonchalance and sophistication. Photo from New York Public Library at Lincoln Center.

Well-known dances that emerged from this era were the jitterbug and the boogie woogie. The boogie woogie was characterized by knee swaying and foot swinging. The jitterbug, initially introduced as the lindy hop (named in honor of aviator Charles Lindbergh), was a syncopated two-step or box step. After the basic step of the lindy, the couples separated for the "breakaway," the improvisational section of the dance. During the middle and late thirties, these improvisations became a show unto themselves. The steps and improvisations of the lindy brought back the solo style of dancing characteristic of African dance and marked a departure from the European style of dancing in couples.

The popularity of jazz dance was promoted around the world in the 1930s by the film industry. The most popular of all dancers during this time was Fred Astaire, with his partner Ginger Rogers. Astaire studied ballet, tap, and ballroom dancing to create a unique style that brought elegance to the dancer's image. He blended the flowing steps of ballet with more-abrupt jazz movements and was the first dancer to actually dance every musical note so that the rhythmic pattern of the music was mirrored in the dance steps. Most of Astaire's dances were performed to songs and music written for musical comedies. His dancing had sophistication, poise, charm, nonchalance, and grace, and it paved the way for a dance style found in jazz dance today.

THE 1940s

Just when the festivity of social jazz dance was at its height, World War II brought a stop to its popularity. Young men were enlisted to serve in battle while young women assisted the war effort in factory and military arms work. Lack of attendance plus the intricate rhythmic patterns of modern jazz music, which were too complex for social dancing, led to the closing of dance halls and ballrooms. With the demise of social jazz dancing, the growth of jazz dance as a professional dance form began. During the 1940s, jazz dance became influenced by ballet and modern dance. By blending the classical technique of ballet with the natural bodily expression of modern dance, jazz dance developed a professional and artistic quality. The formal training necessary to ballet and modern dance was the hitherto missing ingredient that was incorporated into jazz dance at this time. Unlike early jazz dance, which was performed by talented amateurs, modern jazz dance was performed by professionals trained in ballet and modern dance. The dance expertise of these professionals gave rise to the jazz dance of the future. It was at this time that jazz dance as we know it today made its inevitable claim on the Broadway stage and gained the respect of ballet and modern dance choreographers.

In 1943, *Oklahoma*, choreographed by Agnes de Mille, marked the beginning of dance as a major aspect of musical comedy theater. In the years that followed, other ballet choreographers became involved in the production of Broadway musicals. Dance sequences in *Fancy Free* (1944) and *On the Town* (1944), choreographed by Jerome Robbins, incorporated the newer, freer, and more rhythmic form of dance called jazz.

With the increased demand for jazz dance on the stage, it became necessary to develop a more serious and defined jazz dance technique. Jack Cole, trained in modern dance, is often considered the father of jazz dance technique, innovating modern jazz dance movement and technique in the training of professional performers. Cole's technique is concerned with the isolation of body parts and with natural body movement and the flow from one body movement to the next. Besides his work as an innovator of jazz dance technique, Cole is also renowned for his choreography in films and on Broadway; his most famous productions are *Kismet* (1953) and *Man of La Mancha* (1966).

While jazz dance was achieving popularity on the Broadway stage, it continued to make its mark in the film industry with the introduction of Gene Kelly's individual, energetic dance style, which combined athletic and gymnastic abilities with dance. Kelly himself compared his dancing to the feats of an Olympic decathlon champion.

Also at this time, Afro-Haitian, West Indian, and Latin dance forms fused with modern jazz dance, rejuvenating the primitive and earthy style of early jazz dance movements and incorporating a rhythmic

Jerome Robbins' Fancy Free *with ballet star Fernando Bujones. Photo by Martha Swope.*

drumbeat as the primary source of music. Katherine Dunham and Pearl Primus, two black dancers greatly involved in the study of anthropology, researched these areas of dance and contributed their findings to the growing vocabulary of modern jazz dance. Their work created a greater familiarity with, interest in, and respect for the ethnic beginnings of jazz dance. These women also influenced a future generation of black jazz dance choreog-

raphers, including Alvin Ailey, Walter Nicks, and Talley Beatty.

THE 1950s

While in the 1940s jazz dance developed as a professional and disciplined art form, during the late forties and early fifties, the general public did little or no dancing. By 1955, youngsters were be-

Katherine Dunham rekindled interest in African dancing. Photo from New York Public Library at Lincoln Center.

ginning to dance again to the new musical style of rock 'n' roll, a re-creation by white musicians of the kind of music performed by black musicians over the past fifty years. Teenagers now danced in their homes and at record hops to popular music that had a big and often monotonous offbeat. This new beat, which created a widespread rhythmic revolution, was extremely danceable and tailored for the jukebox and home phonograph. Rock 'n'

roll was promoted by record companies and popularized by local disc jockeys. The financial impact of rock 'n' roll on the nation was apparent—new sources of income were created by American preteen and teenage consumers.

Rock 'n' roll also had a social impact on the nation. Adolescents used their phonographs, loud-playing songs, and dance movements that adults found grotesque as a means for protest and rebellion. Surprisingly, however, these new dances were throwbacks to earlier eras. The chicken was a parody of the lindy; the mashed potato was reminiscent of the charleston; and the jitterbug was popular at all the sock hops.

Elvis Presley's arrival on the scene in 1956 transformed rock 'n' roll. Presley popularized a blend of hillbilly, gospel, blues, and popular music and introduced rock 'n' roll to the TV screen. The popularity of the music spread the popularity of dancing, and such television shows as *American Bandstand* became nationally successful by presenting teenagers dancing to popular music.

While dance prospered on the social dance floor, professional jazz dance continued to gain respect, as evidenced by its increasing use on stage and in films. In 1951, Jerome Robbins choreographed the film *An American in Paris*, starring Gene Kelly. In 1957, the American public recognized jazz dance as never before with a landmark in American musical theater—*West Side Story*, with choreography by Robbins and music by Leonard Bernstein. The choreography of *West Side Story* captured the style of New York's "cool" West Side ghetto youths in the pimp's walk, a step originating in the black bottom and characterized by a leaning at the waist, shoulders elevated, knees lifted high, and fingers snapping. The use of jazz dancing on the Broadway stage continued with contributions from jazz choreographers Michael Kidd, Peter Gennaro, and Gower Champion.

The exciting jazz ballet from West Side Story, *choreographed by Jerome Robbins. Photo by Martha Swope.*

Through the fifties and into the sixties, many dancers who turned teacher/choreographer contributed to the development of jazz dance and the emerging variety of jazz dance styles. Thus began the serious study by professional dancers of this newly accepted dance form. During this period of development in jazz dance, Matt Mattox emerged as a major talent. Much of Mattox's technique is dedicated to the development of isolation of body parts. Mattox, who was greatly influenced by Jack

Cole, views the body in its simplest form as a straight line (a concept Mattox may have developed from Cole's interest and study of the linear design of East Indian dance). Seeing the body as a straight line, Mattox studied the infinite number of designs that could be made with the body. The Mattox style is percussive, with strong angular movements and sharp accents, rebounds, and turns. Mattox's first choreography was *Say Darling* in 1958. His career continued with choreography for other Broadway shows, the Metropolitan Opera Ballet, *The Bell Telephone Hour*, and the New Jersey Ballet Company.

THE 1960s

The early 1960s introduced the twist. The twist, characterized by Presley-like hip gyrations, partners never touching but responding to each other's movements, brought adults back to the social dance floor and became an overnight fad, an international craze, because it was so easy to perform. A second wave of dances followed the twist: the frug—a takeoff on the shimmy—and a series of dances that were pantomimes with hand and arm gestures and little footwork or body motion— the hitchhiker, the monkey, and the swim. The jerk was another popular dance influenced by the bumps and grinds of Elvis Presley.

The teenage population was attracted to the dance floor by the immense popularity of the Beatles' music, which was extremely danceable, incorporating a variety of rhythms and interesting, relevant lyrics. The hippie, "flower child" years of the late sixties brought a new style of rock music influenced by psychedelic drugs and political protest, and a revival of old dance halls—now the scene of live rock music, psychedelic light shows, and solo improvisatory dancing.

Matt Mattox views the body as a straight line and then sees what designs can come from it. Photo from New York Public Library at Lincoln Center.

With the increased popularity of social dancing, discotheques—nightclubs featuring dancing to recorded music—emerged. By 1965, there were five thousand discotheques in America. Dance studios also flourished as dance enthusiasts attempted to keep abreast of dance fads that came and went from week to week.

Television shows now featured music and

among the ranks of professional jazz dance greats: Eugene Louis Facciuto—or "Luigi," as he is affectionately called—and Gus Giordano. Both of these men have achieved continuing fame as developers of jazz dance technique and choreography.

Luigi's technique was developed as a result of an auto accident that left him paralyzed on the right side. Although doctors claimed he would never walk, let alone dance, again, Luigi persisted with operations, physical therapy, and his own study of body development based on dance exercise and attained the ability to move and dance again. His renewed study of dance earned him performances in many films and choreography credits on Broadway, in Hollywood, and in nightclub shows in Reno and Las Vegas. Luigi has approached dance movement by developing a systematic series of exercises using the total body in each movement phrase. His technique requires that the body be exercised to its fullest to develop the strength necessary for muscle control, yet still look beautiful. The Luigi technique, influenced by ballet training, is lyrical in style and can best be seen in detail in his own book, *Jazz with Luigi.*

Luigi believes the body should be used to its fullest.

professional dancing; most notable of these were *Shindig, Hullabaloo,* and certain sequences of *Laugh-In.* Television gave popular dance crazes a broad appeal and also professionalized these dances by refining them into choreographed routines with professional solo and chorus performers. The market for these shows gave dancers a steady income and expanded the alternatives for a dance career.

During the sixties, two major names appeared

Gus Giordano is prominent in the Midwest and nationally respected for his technique and choreography. His performance credits include appearances on *The Dean Martin–Jerry Lewis Show, The Ed Sullivan Show,* and *The Perry Como Show.* Although Giordano's style is classical, it is greatly influenced by the natural and freer body movements of modern dance. His technique teaches isolation movements, emphasizing the head and torso and creating an uplifted look of elegance. Yoga is incorporated into his technique as a means of relaxation. Among his major credits for choreography is "Requiem for a Slave," which won an Emmy award. Further study of Gus Giordano may be made through his book *Anthology of American Jazz Dance.*

The Gus Giordano Jazz Dance Chicago troupe. Giordano's technique is influenced by the natural and free body movements of modern dance. Photo by John Randolph.

THE 1970s

In the 1970s, the public was more receptive to a broad variety of entertainment forms, as can be seen in the wide range of musical and dance styles that appeared at this time. College students were attending rock concerts, aspiring musicians played free concerts in city parks, while folk music was being heard in restaurant lounges. Musical tastes ranged from acid rock to electronic music to soul and lyrical jazz. Discotheques (now called discos) gave rise to such choreographed line dances as the bus stop, the roller coaster, and the hustle. The bump, another popular dance, encouraged bodily contact as partners bumped one another with various parts of their anatomy.

At the theater, the public fell in love with Michael Bennett's *A Chorus Line* (1975) and Bob Fosse's *Chicago* (1975). Dance as the primary theme of a production was now able to capture the attention of a Broadway crowd.

In the seventies, Bob Fosse became the outstanding name in jazz dance. Although he has worked as a performer on Broadway and in films, Fosse's true success is as a choreographer, beginning with his first choreography, *Pajama Game*, in 1954, and followed by *Damn Yankees* (1955), *Bells Are Ringing* (1956), *New Girl in Town* (1957), *Redhead* (1959), *Little*

Bob Fosse's Tony award–winning show Dancin'. *Fosse's dances are slick and entertaining. Photo by Martha Swope.*

Me (1962), and *Sweet Charity* (1967). In 1973, Fosse was the first director in history to win three national entertainment awards: the Oscar for his film version of *Cabaret*, the Tony for the Broadway musical *Pippin*, and the Emmy for the television special *Liza with a Z.* In 1978, Fosse received a second Tony award for his Broadway success *Dancin'*. Drawing on his varied talents, Fosse also directed, co-authored, and choreographed the widely acclaimed and Oscar-nominated film *All That Jazz* (1979).

The Fosse name connotes a distinct jazz style. He is highly creative, with unusual, individualized, and often bizarre movements. His choreography is extremely slick and erotic and displays a great intensity. There are many characteristic poses that are identifiable as the Fosse style; most recognizable is the long-legged look with raised arm and limp wrist. Fosse and his highly personalized jazz dance style are certain to continue to make a mark on the Broadway stage and in Hollywood films throughout the 1980s.

THE 1980s

The 1980s present jazz dance in all the variety of its forms—on the Broadway stage, on the concert stage, in films, on television specials and variety shows, and even in commercials.

Although jazz dance has undergone many changes since its beginning, it continues to be influenced by the music and social dances characteristic of the era. The music that was popular in the 1970s has continued, but the eighties have added new wave and punk rock. These musical styles are intended more to make a social comment than merely to entertain. The musicians as well as their music focus on the irrational and evoke the bizarre. Punk rock is hard rock with the heavy use of electronic sounds and rebellious lyrics. New wave is characterized by a primitive beat and repetitive musical phrases and lyrics. Dances that have evolved from this music are the pogo and slam dancing. In both, the dancers jump around with uncontrolled body movements. In slam dancing, the main intent is to slam into other dancers on the dance floor.

The 1980s are also the age of technological advancement and computer science. The computer was originally used primarily in business and scientific research, but its scope has expanded to the educational field, entertainment games (video games), and even to choreography. The science of the human body and the knowledge of its potential have also greatly expanded.

Increased public consciousness of the health hazards in our environment and the problems brought by unsound nutritional habits and sedentary lifestyles has encouraged people to seek a new, more physical lifestyle and has promoted exercise as a social function. People more than ever before are seeking a form of fitness that is not only good for their health but is also fun. This social and physical need has made jazz dance extremely popular in the 1980s. This popularity is understandable. Jazz dance is now a dance form that everyone can participate in. It is an excellent form of exercise that not only conditions the body but also stimulates the mind and aesthetic sense. The upbeat tempo of the music that is an integral part of all classes provides motivation, maintains interest, and creates a social atmosphere in a fitness activity enjoyed by men and women alike.

Jazz dance throughout the 1980s will continue to be influenced by the advancements of today's technological age and the scientific study of the human body. In addition, jazz music will continue to change and exert its influence upon jazz dance. The influences of other dance forms (ballet, modern, ethnic, tap, and social dance) on jazz dance will continue to build on its variety and keep it versatile, contemporary, and exciting.

Now, let's jump into jazz!

Chapter 2

Getting Started

Most students enrolled in a jazz dance class for the first time need some initiation in what to wear and how to present themselves in class. Although specific requirements will vary, there are some basic conventions in dress, appearance, and etiquette that the student should know. This chapter discusses these common conventions and also outlines the basic structure of a jazz dance lesson.

The Gus Giordano Jazz Dance Chicago troupe. Styles of jazz attire vary with the individual. Photo by Jack Mitchell, New York City.

ATTIRE

Dance is perceived as a series of designs in space, created through body positions and movements. It is therefore essential that dance clothing reveal body line and allow freedom of movement.

The primary focus of the beginning jazz dance student is the imitation of the instructor's positions and movements, with special attention given to body alignment and placement (see Chapter 3, "A Dancer's Posture"). Wearing the proper clothing will enable your instructor to check your body line and will help you check yourself in the studio mirror.

Women's Clothing

Women generally wear a leotard and tights. Stirrup tights with toe and heel open may be preferred because they can be worn with or without shoes. Underwear is generally not worn beneath the tights because its outline shows below the line of the leotard and disrupts the long, smooth look of the leg.

With the rising popularity of dancewear as street clothing, a variety of leotard styles, colors, and fabrics is now available. In most jazz dance classes, students are free to create their own clothing ensembles. However, it is advisable to first check with the instructor regarding dress code.

Men's Clothing

Men's clothing also consists of leotard and tights. The tights may be regular or stirrup style and are made of a heavier material than that of women's tights. A dance belt is worn under the tights and serves the same purpose as an athletic supporter. The dance belt gives more support, however, as it is constructed for the variety of stretching, jumping, and leg-lifting activities performed in dance.

Although men wear leotards in styles cut for the male body, they wear their tights atop the leotards. The tights are held up either by a belt or elastic around the waist, over which the tights are rolled, or by clip-on suspenders.

In addition to the essential dress items of leotard and tights, both men and women often wear leg or ankle warmers, sweater tops, jazz pants, or jazz unitards. Since the dancer's muscles perform best when they are warm, these items are often worn to accelerate the rise in body heat during initial class activities.

Footwear

Depending upon the type of dance studio floor, shoes may or may not be required. If shoes are worn in class, students may want to try the leather or canvas jazz shoe, the jazz sandal, or the suede-strapped sandal shoe. Some instructors may also allow ballet or gymnastic shoes. "Character shoes" are often worn by women for auditions or performances but are not usually recommended for class lessons.

APPEARANCE

Good grooming habits are as essential for the dance classroom as they are in daily life. The hair should be secured away from the face so that it is not bothersome. Excessive jewelry should not be worn, for it distracts from the body line and can disrupt dance movements or injure other dancers. Elastic straps to secure eyeglasses in place are encouraged. If a student perspires heavily, it is appropriate to bring a small towel to use during lesson breaks.

ETIQUETTE

The basic rules of etiquette for the dance classroom promote consideration for other dancers and allow the class to proceed smoothly and rapidly, without interruption and delay. The student should arrive on time or early for the dance lesson. Arriving late is not only rude to the instructor, it is also harmful to the dancer, for it hurries the body into vigorous exercise without a proper warm-up and may result in serious injury. At no time should a student enter a classroom with food, drink, or chewing gum. Other considerate behavior should include no unnecessary talking or interruption of the instructor during the instruction period. Most teachers will ask for questions at appropriate intervals.

When locomotor movements or dance combinations are performed across the floor, a line is generally formed at either one side or one corner of the room. Students move with a partner, in fours, or in a group number assigned by the teacher. As you approach the front of the line, you should assemble with your partner or group quickly and be ready to move at the start of your turn. You should not stop a dance combination midway across the floor, because the group of dancers immediately following you would be disrupted. When you complete your turn, it is proper etiquette to walk around the perimeter of the room to return to the end of the line.

When dance combinations are to be performed in the center of the floor, the student should stand in an area where the instructor is either directly visible or visible in the mirror. As the center dance combinations are performed, the student should be aware of the movement space and should not intrude into the space of other students.

At the close of the dance lesson, students usually applaud in unison. This applause expresses appreciation both for the instruction the teacher has given and for the efforts and performances of fellow students.

BASIC STRUCTURE OF A JAZZ DANCE LESSON

Although all instructors will have their own personal lesson formats, the following activities are characteristic of a jazz dance lesson.

Pre–Warm-up

Many lessons begin with pre–warm-up exercises—very simple and slow body movements that align and prime the body for the warm-up exercises that follow. Many teachers will expect students to begin this part of the lesson on their own, which is why an early arrival to class is encouraged.

Warm-up

Warm-up exercises stimulate blood circulation to the muscles by progressive movements that gradually stretch, strengthen, align, and coordinate the body. Warm-up exercises are done in a variety of positions—standing, at the *barre*,* sitting, or lying on the floor. Included in the warm-up may be exercises for the development of basic dance technique. The warm-up may also introduce specific jazz movements that will later be incorporated into dance combinations. Isolation movements, an integral part of jazz dance, are often performed during the warm-up.

---

*barre: a long, horizontal wooden bar, attached to the wall or freestanding, used for support and balance.

Isolation Movements

Isolation exercises train the dancer to isolate and move one body part through its possible positions. Instructors sometimes combine various isolation movements so that two or more body parts move at the same time, thus helping the student develop coordination. Students may perform isolation exercises while standing or while moving across the floor.

Locomotor Movements

At the conclusion of the warm-up period, locomotor combinations are presented. This part of the lesson is usually the first opportunity for the student to perform dance steps. Locomotor, or "across the floor," movements stress the technical approach to dance steps and may introduce movement sequences that will later be presented in a dance combination.

Dance Combinations

In the jazz dance class, the culmination of the lesson is the learning and performing of a dance combination—a combination of movements utilizing all the elements of dance and testing the dancer's technique, coordination, and memory.

The instructor will demonstrate the movement patterns of the dance combination in short sequences, explaining the counts, the spatial direction, and the proper techniques of executing specific steps. When the students have learned the dance steps and are able to execute the transitions from one movement to the next, the music for the performance of the combination is introduced. At this point, the class is generally divided into smaller groups that present the combination alternately. Students can learn from their own performances and also from watching other dancers perform. Students should observe carefully the flow of the movements, the transitions between steps, the exact positions of the body, the timing of intricate steps, and the style of performance.

Throughout the lesson, the instructor will give general corrections to the class as a whole and sometimes specific criticisms to individual students. Constructive criticism is offered to assist the student in learning the techniques of dance quickly and correctly. Dance students should practice outside of class, utilizing the corrections given in lessons. Often there is a progression of dance steps and combinations from one class to the next. The student who practices the combinations outside of class will experience the greatest and quickest progress.

Chapter 3

A Dancer's Posture

The dancer's body should present an image of grace and elegant carriage. The reason for this image is more than just aesthetic. What is perceived as an elegant and graceful carriage is actually the correct skeletal alignment necessary in dance for maximum balance and ease of movement. This chapter describes correct posture and body alignment for the dancer and presents exercises to help the student make correct alignment second nature.

Dancin' *by Bob Fosse. Notice the different postures. Photo by Martha Swope.*

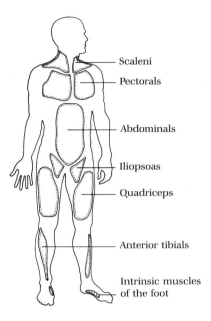

Figure 3-1 General Location of Postural Muscles: Front View

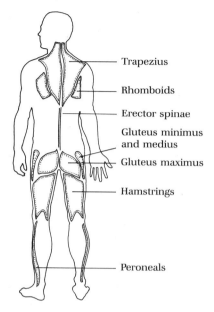

Figure 3-2 General Location of Postural Muscles: Rear View

POSTURE AND ALIGNMENT

The term *alignment*, as used in dance, refers to the relationship of the body segments to one another and to the pull of gravity. When the body is in correct vertical alignment, the pull of gravity can be utilized to its greatest advantage, with a minimum of strain on the muscles and ligaments attached to the weight-bearing joints.

Correct alignment is essential for all dancers, novice or professional. It helps the dancer achieve the maximum in balance, coordination, and freedom of movement. Without correct alignment, the dancer will be unable to balance and will experience early muscle fatigue and possibly injury. It is

for these reasons that alignment should be one of the first skills a dancer acquires.

Certain *postural muscles*, termed antigravity muscles, automatically work to keep the body upright (see Figures 3-1 and 3-2). However, since the skeletal structure is not exactly vertical, the dancer must develop an additional conscious control of these muscles to achieve the alignment necessary for efficient movement and balance. Correct alignment depends on a balanced relationship between the anterior (front) and the posterior (back) postural muscles. An imbalance in the relationship between these muscles will result in postural deviations.

Figure 3-3   Correct Alignment: Side View

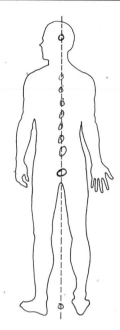

Figure 3-4   Correct Alignment: Rear View

ALIGNMENT REFERENCE POINTS

Although each individual body structure may have minor variations, visual guidelines do exist for evaluating correct alignment.

In a side view of correct alignment, an imaginary line of gravity passes through the following body reference points (see Figure 3-3):

1. The front of the ankle bone
2. The back of the knee cap
3. The center of the hip
4. The middle of the shoulder
5. Behind the top of the ear

In a back view of correct alignment, an imaginary line of gravity passes through the following body reference points (see Figure 3-4):

1. Midway between the heels
2. Through the cleft of the buttocks
3. Through the midpoint of all vertebrae
4. Through the center of the head

PLACEMENT

The term *placement*, as used in dance, refers to the proper positioning of the separate body parts in order to achieve total correct body alignment (see

Figures 3-5 and 3-6). The student should become familiar with the proper placement of the major body parts described below—the pelvis, rib cage, shoulder girdle, head and neck, feet, and knees—and should use the studio mirror to go through a mental checklist of their proper placement in all positions and movements. With practice, the student will develop an inner awareness of proper placement without the aid of a mirror, and eventually proper placement will become second nature.

The Pelvis

The pelvis is the keystone of the skeleton. The tilt of the pelvis affects the posture of the entire body and the distribution of body weight over the feet. Correct placement of the pelvis is in a centered position, allowing a lengthening of the lumbar spine and a shortening of the abdominal muscles. Extreme forward or backward tilting of the pelvis can injure the lumbar spine and the muscles of the lower back. Alignment exercises 1 and 2 below will allow the student to experience the proper placement of the pelvis.

The Rib Cage

The rib cage floats above the pelvis and is connected in back to the spinal column. The rib cage should be pulled in toward the spine and lifted upward from the pelvis, to create a long-waisted appearance. Alignment exercise 8 will allow the student to experience the proper placement of the rib cage.

The Shoulder Girdle

The shoulder girdle—consisting of the collar bones in front and the shoulder blades in back—should

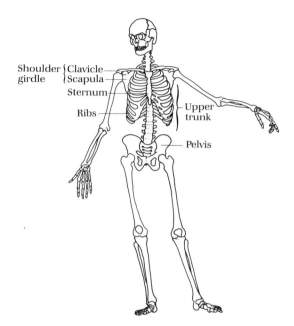

Figure 3-5 Skeletal Structures Important to Correct Placement: Front View

Shoulder girdle { Clavicle / Scapula
Sternum
Ribs
Upper trunk
Pelvis

be placed directly above the rib cage. The shoulder girdle is attached to the trunk only at the sternum (breastbone), allowing it to move freely. The shoulders should not be pulled back or allowed to slump forward; rather, they should point directly to the side resulting in an equal openness of the chest and the shoulder blades. The arms should hang freely in the shoulder sockets. The shoulders should be lowered and the neck lengthened to increase the distance between the shoulders and the ears. Alignment exercises 6 and 7 will allow the student to experience the proper placement of the shoulder girdle.

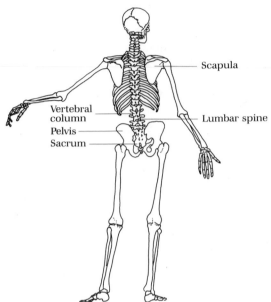

Figure 3-6 Skeletal Structures Important to Correct Placement: Rear View

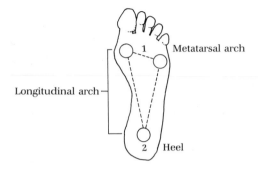

Figure 3-7 Weight-Bearing Areas in the Foot

allow the student to experience the proper placement of the head and neck.

The Feet

Although the pelvis is the keystone of the skeletal structure, the feet provide the main base of support. In a static position, the greatest support is achieved when the weight of the body is equally distributed over the metatarsal arch (the ball of the foot), the base of the big toe, the base of the small toe, and the heel (see Figure 3-7). All of the toes should remain in contact with the floor to provide the widest possible base of support. In addition, the longitudinal arch should be well lifted to prevent the ankle from rolling inward.

The Knees

Finally, the knee position, which is affected by the placement of the pelvis, should be directly above and in line with the direction of the toes. In the standing position, the knees should be slightly relaxed. Hyperextension (a locking or pressing too far back) of the knees is a common error.

The Head and Neck

The head, the heaviest body segment, rests on the neck, which is a small, flexible segment. The head should be carried directly atop the neck, protruding neither forward nor backward. With the head in this position, the chin should be held parallel to the floor. There should be a sense of the neck stretching away from the spine so that both the back and the front of the neck will be long. With the head and neck in correct alignment, a vertical line can be drawn from the top of the ear to the middle of the shoulder. Alignment exercise 5 will

ALIGNMENT EXERCISES

Outlined below are exercises to help the dancer achieve correct body alignment. These exercises may easily be performed in ten minutes and can serve as a pre–warm-up to dance class. It is recommended that they be performed daily until correct alignment becomes a habit.

Starting Position for Exercises.   Lie on the back, with knees bent, soles of the feet flat on the ground, arms by the side of the body, and the palms of both hands flat on the floor.

Exercise 1: Placement of the Pelvis.   Assume the starting position and take deep breaths. As you exhale, allow the stomach to contract so that the lower back is in total contact with the floor. Hold this position, concentrating on the position of the lower back and stomach. Repeat the exercise four times. Maintain the position of the lower back against the floor throughout the remaining exercises.

Exercise 2: Placement of the Pelvis.   Assume the starting position, maintaining the alignment of the lower back as achieved in exercise 1. Slowly stretch the arms on the floor above the head and hold the stretched position several seconds, maintaining the lower back against the floor. Relax and release the back to allow the natural curve of the spine. With the arms in the stretched position, straighten the legs along the floor. Hold this position for several seconds, maintaining the lower back against the floor. Return to the starting position. Repeat the exercise four times.

Exercise 3: Tightening the Abdominal Muscles and Lengthening the Lumbar Spine. Assume the starting position with the hands clasped behind the neck. Lift the head and right knee as you lift the left elbow to touch the right knee. As the elbow and knee touch, exhale and contract the stomach. Return to starting position. Repeat with the opposite elbow and knee. Repeat the exercise eight times on each side. Concentrate on contracting the stomach muscles as the elbow and knee touch.

Exercise 4: Tightening the Abdominal Muscles and Lengthening the Lumbar Spine. Assume the starting position with the hands clasped behind the neck. Lift the head and both knees off the floor, bringing the elbows forward to touch the lifted bent knees. Slowly lower both head and knees to the starting position, checking that the spine sequentially resumes contact with the floor. Repeat the exercise slowly eight times.

Exercise 5: Placement of the Head and Neck. Assume the starting position with hands clasped behind the head (not the neck). Lift the head only off the floor and pull the elbows together. A stretch at the base of the neck and all down the spine should be felt. Slowly place the head back on the floor, stretching the neck away from the spine. Repeat this stretch three times. Maintain this neck alignment throughout the remaining exercises.

Exercise 6: Placement of the Shoulder Girdle. Assume the starting position and place both hands on the hip bones. Keeping the elbows in contact with the floor, use an isometric (static) stretch to point the elbows toward the sides of the room. Hold for ten seconds, then relax. Repeat this stretch four times. Although the movement of this exercise is slight, when executed properly it will equally expand the back and the chest. Maintain this back and chest expansion throughout the remaining exercises.

Exercise 7: Placement of the Shoulder Girdle. Assume the starting position, with the hands placed on the hip bones. Isolate the shoulders by lifting them forward off the floor. Hold this position for five seconds. Relax and place the shoulders in total contact with the floor. As this exercise is performed, attempt to create the greatest distance possible between the shoulders and the ears. This will help to maintain the correct shoulder and neck alignment. Repeat the exercise four times.

Exercise 8: Placement of the Rib Cage. Assume the starting position, with the hands on the hip bones. Lift the rib cage forward off the floor to create an extreme arch in the back. Reverse the action, pressing the rib cage back against the floor, or further toward the spine. Repeat the exercise four times, ending with the rib cage in its correct placement against the floor.

End this brief exercise session in the final position achieved in exercise 8. Mentally review the correct alignment of the body parts:

1. The lower back is flat against the floor.
2. The stomach is contracted and hollowed out.
3. The back and the chest are open and equally expanded, with the elbows pointing to the side.
4. The neck and ears are stretching away from the spine and the shoulders.
5. The shoulders are resting flat against the floor.
6. Breathing is full and easy.

Once the proper body placement is attained on the floor, attempt to achieve the same correct alignment in the standing position. Once correct alignment is attained in the standing position, attempt to maintain this alignment while walking and performing dance movements.

Chapter 4

Ballet for the Jazz Dancer

Classical ballet training develops line and form (the two- and three-dimensional images created by the dancer's body), muscle strength, joint flexibility, balance, and coordination. Ballet training is valuable to the jazz dancer because it provides a basic understanding of dance principles and instills the proper execution of dance techniques. Ballet techniques, positions, movements, and vocabulary typically included in the jazz dance class are outlined in this chapter.

Ballet's principles and techniques developed in the seventeenth century and were founded on classical ideals of grace and beauty. The line and form

Gus Giordano Jazz Dance Chicago. Ballet training is important for the jazz dancer. Photo by Jack Mitchell, New York City.

of Greek statues provided an inspiration for early choreographers, who developed a technique based upon their study and understanding of the body. Through the years, the classical ideals of ballet have been maintained, but technical discoveries have aided the advancement of its technique.

The terminology defined in this chapter is in standard use in both ballet and jazz dance. Because ballet developed in France, the terms used are in French; since they describe the movements literally, we have included English translations to help the student better understand the essence of the particular movement. Dance combinations are built from these basic positions and movements, so the student should be familiar with the basic vocabulary in order to follow the teacher's instructions.

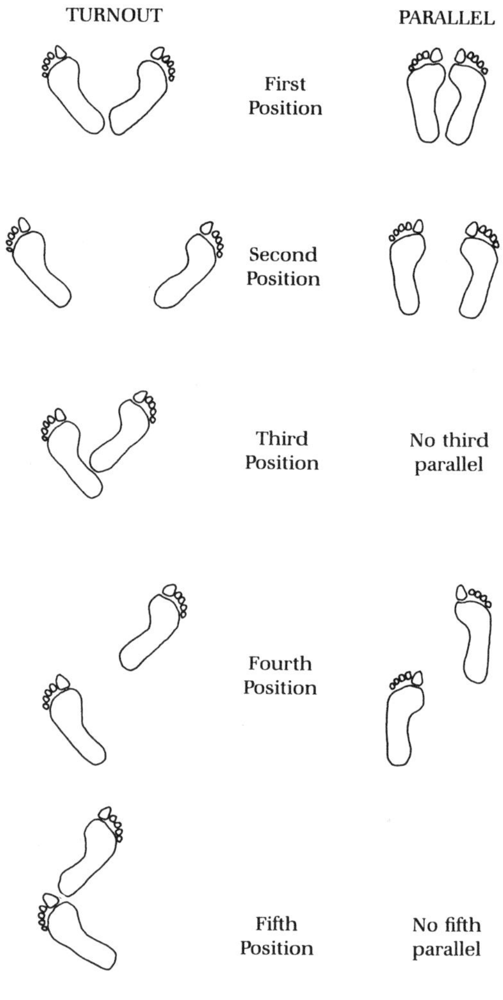

TURNOUT

PARALLEL

First
Position

Second
Position

Third
Position

No third
parallel

Fourth
Position

Fifth
Position

No fifth
parallel

Figure 4-1 Positions of the Feet

TURNOUT

Turnout is the outward rotation of the legs from the hip sockets. The turned-out position maximizes the dancer's balance because it provides a wider base of support than does a parallel position (Figure 4-1). Turnout also reveals more of the dancer's leg, gives a slimmer side view of the dancer, and facilitates sideward movement.

The degree of turnout is defined by the skeletal structure of the pelvic girdle and by the muscles controlling the rotation of the leg at the hip socket. To determine your natural turnout, stand with your feet in parallel first position (Figure 4-1). In one movement, rotate the legs outward from the hip joints. The end position, without additional movement of the feet, is your natural turnout. A common error is to turn the feet out farther than the legs are actually turned out at the hip joints—a practice that can result in injury to the muscles and ligaments of the hip, knee, and ankle joints. The range of turnout can be increased with flexibility exercises for the muscles surrounding the hip joint and strength-building exercises for the muscles that rotate the legs outward.

POSITIONS OF THE FEET

In ballet, all movements proceed from, and end in, the five basic positions of the feet, which are executed in turnout. In jazz dance, these positions are executed in turnout and parallel. The contrasting positions are shown in Figure 4-1.

POSITIONS OF THE ARMS

Ballet has also defined five positions of the arms, with slight variations depending on the origin of training. These arm positions correspond to and balance the foot positions. In all positions, a specific manner of holding the arms is used to create the graceful ballet line: The arms are held slightly rounded and slightly forward of the body, with the shoulders down and relaxed; the wrist and hand are held as an extension of the arm, with the thumb held inward toward the palm and the fingers relaxed.

First Position

The arms are held slightly rounded at the side.

Second Position

The arms are held horizontally and slightly rounded.

Third Position

One arm is held slightly rounded to the side and midway between first and second positions. The other arm is held in fifth position low.

Fourth Position

One arm is held in second position. The other arm may be held in either fifth position front or fifth position high.

Fifth Position

There are three fifth positions:

Fifth Position Low. The arms are held slightly rounded in front of the thighs.

Fifth Position Front. The arms are held slightly rounded in front of the chest, parallel to the floor.

Fifth Position High. The arms are held slightly rounded over the head.

In jazz dance, the arm is often straight, with the fingers spread wide open (the *jazz hand*).

BALLET MOVEMENTS

All ballet movements are performed in the turned-out position. To maintain turnout during leg movements, certain rules should be followed:

1. When the leg is extended to the front, the heel leads the movement and continually presses forward to maintain the turned-out position of the leg.
2. When the leg is extended to the side, the heel presses forward as the leg extends on the diagonal line of the turnout.
3. When the leg is extended to the rear, the toe leads the movement, while the heel presses forward, maintaining the turned-out position of the leg. The pelvis should face squarely front.

In jazz dance, the ballet movements described below are also performed in the parallel position.

Plié

The *plié* ("bend") is a smooth and continuous bending and straightening of the knees. The legs are turned out at the hip joints, allowing the thighs and knees to open directly above the line of the toes.

There are two *pliés*, the *demi-plié* and the *grand plié*. The *demi-plié* is a half-bending of the knees without lifting the heels from the floor. The *grand plié* is a full bending of the knees, passing through the *demi-plié* and continuing to lower the body until only the balls of the feet remain on the floor (except in second position, in which the heels never leave the floor). In straightening the legs from the *grand plié*, it is essential to pass through the *demi-plié*, returning the heels to the floor before regaining the full vertical position.

The *demi-plié* and the *grand plié* are executed in all positions with the weight evenly distributed over both feet and the torso held erect.

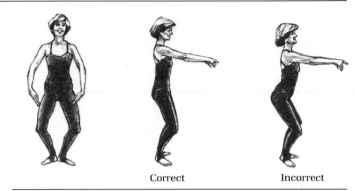

Correct   Incorrect

Correct   Incorrect

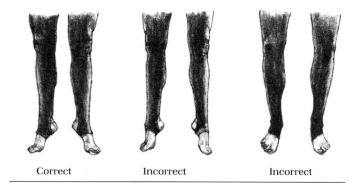

Correct   Incorrect   Incorrect

Relevé

The *relevé* ("rise") is a rise onto the balls of the feet, with the legs straight and the torso held erect. The weight of the body must be centered between the first and second toes to maintain correct alignment of the ankle. The toes should be extended and spread open against the floor for balance. The upper body is lifted as the balls of the feet press into the floor on the rise, and it remains lifted as the heels are lowered to the floor on the descent.

Battements

A *battement* ("beating") is an extension of the leg that brushes the foot along the floor. *Battements* can be performed to the front, side, or back. The level of the leg and the quality of the movement define the type of *battement*.

Battement Tendu. The *battement tendu* ("stretched beating") is a brush of the straight leg to its full extension, with only the toes remaining on the floor. The foot must release contact with the floor in a sequential movement from the heel through the ball of the foot to the toes. The closing of the *tendu* reverses the sequential movement.

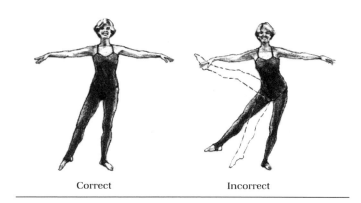

Correct   Incorrect

Correct

Battement Dégagé. The *battement dégagé* ("released beating") is a quick brush of the straight leg through *tendu* to a position slightly off the floor. The rapidity of this movement trains the foot to work quickly; it is therefore essential that the foot is not lifted higher than four inches off the floor.

Grand Battement. The *grand battement* ("large beating") is a high, straight leg lift, passing through the *tendu* and *dégagé* and carrying the leg quickly to ninety degrees or higher. The return of the *grand battement* passes through the closing movement of the *tendu*. Lifting the leg quickly and lowering it slowly is an essential technique in *grand battement*.

Arabesque

The *arabesque* takes its name from a form of Moorish ornament. In this position, the body is supported on one leg, which may be straight or in *demi-plié*, while the other leg is fully extended to the rear and raised as high as possible against the back. The arms are held in various harmonious positions, usually with one arm extended forward to create a long straight line from the fingertips of the extended front arm to the toes of the extended leg. The hips and shoulders should remain square to the direction the body is facing, and the upper torso should be held upright, although as the extended leg is raised to greater heights, the body may lean slightly forward to maintain the long straight line.

Attitude

The *attitude* (a pose) is thought to be derived from the statue of Mercury by Giovanni da Bologna. It is a balance position on one leg, with the opposite leg extended, knee bent, to the front, side, or rear. The thigh of the bent leg is parallel to the floor, and the toe is as high as, or slightly below, the height of the knee.

Passé

The *passé* ("passed through") is a balance position on one leg, with the opposite leg bent and the toe pointed to touch the hollow of the knee of the standing leg. When the *passé* is performed in turnout, the standing leg and the bent knee are turned out as far as possible. In jazz dance, the *passé* is also executed in the parallel position, with the knees of both legs pointing straight ahead and the foot of the bent leg pressed firmly against the knee of the standing leg.

PRINCIPLES OF MOVEMENT

In both ballet and jazz dance, certain principles of movement must be applied at all times. The dance student should continually work on these principles until their execution becomes automatic.

Shift of Weight

When the body shifts support from both feet to one foot, or from one foot to the other, a shift of weight must also occur. If balance is to be maintained, the shift of weight must occur without a change in the alignment of the pelvis, which should remain horizontal throughout the movement. Pulling in and up on the stomach muscles will keep the pelvis in its correct position and the weight lifted out of the legs, thus enabling a smooth shift of weight.

Correct   Incorrect

Jumps

The ability to jump high and land softly and smoothly demands the application of important ballet principles. These principles not only help to achieve a beautiful and exciting jump, they are also necessary in preventing injury to the dancer's knees, ankles, and feet.

There are four principles that must be applied when performing jumps of any kind:

1. The dancer must begin all jumps from the *demi-plié* position.
2. To attain the height of the jump, the dancer must press off the floor through a full extension (pointing) of the feet.
3. The dancer must land from the jump on the balls of the feet, rolling through to the heels.
4. All jumps must end with a return to the *demi-plié* position.

Turns

Spectators are always entranced with the dancer's ability to turn, and beginning dancers are always amazed at how dizzy they become when first attempting to turn. The secret to alleviating this dizziness and acquiring the ability to do multiple turns is *spotting*. Spotting is the ability of the dancer to keep the eyes focused on one spot as long as possible while turning the body. When eye contact on the focus spot can no longer be maintained, the dancer quickly turns the head, immediately regaining focus on the chosen spot, which should be at, or slightly above, eye level. It is best to start the practice of spotting by executing a walking turn slowly in place, gradually increasing the speed until the whip of the head is quick and smooth and the eyes focus quickly.

Other ballet terms are often used in jazz dance, but the movements they describe are usually performed in the jazz style. These movements and their new jazz names will be included in Chapter 5, "Basic Jazz Dance."

Chapter 5

Basic Jazz Dance

Ballet developed in an academic situation in which a vocabulary was defined by classic ideals of beauty and grace and enlarged as technical discoveries concerning flexibility, strength, elevation, and turns advanced. Jazz dance, in contrast, was developed through improvisation and through the personalities and styles of its performers. This process made a clear-cut vocabulary for jazz dance nearly impossible. In spite of this problem, and even though each school of jazz dance has its own unique set of movements as created by the instructor, certain positions and steps have become a universally accepted jazz dance vocabulary. This chapter attempts to define and describe these basic jazz movements. However, it must be understood that, unlike a ballet dictionary in which every known step is included, this list is just a sampling of the most basic steps that the student is likely to encounter in the beginning jazz dance class.

BODY POSITIONS

Certain basic positions are used continually throughout a jazz dance class. These positions are used during the warm-up as well as in combinations to create variety in locomotor movements. It is important when first learning these positions to

Liz Williamson, America's queen of jazz dance, lives and teaches in New York City. Photo by Jack Mitchell, New York City.

execute them precisely so that their accurate execution will become habit. Do not hesitate to use a mirror to check your position.

Arch

| Correct | Incorrect | Correct | Incorrect |

The *arch* position of the spine is a curve of the torso upward and backward. Since the movement is a curve of the entire spine, the head is a part of the curve and is not dropped against the back. It is important in the arch position to contract the buttocks and stomach muscles so that there is limited use of the lower back.

Contraction

| Correct | Incorrect |

The term *contraction* indicates a drawing in or shortening of body parts. Although the term may refer to any body part, in jazz, contraction often refers to the torso. In a torso contraction, the front of the torso is concave so that a "C" curve of the spine is formed. The lower back is rounded, pulling the pelvis forward, and the stomach is hollowed, with the shoulders held directly above the hips. The chest and shoulders should not slump.

Flat Back

Flat back is a position in which the dancer bends forward from the hips at a ninety-degree angle. The back is straight and parallel to the floor. Flat back is also referred to as *tabletop position*.

Diagonal Flat Back

In the *diagonal flat back* position, the dancer bends from the hips until the straight back is parallel to the floor and then shifts the torso sideways until it is diagonal to the direction in which the legs are facing. Both sides of the body must maintain equal stretch in this position.

Hinge

A *hinge* is a tilt of the torso with an imaginary oblique straight line that passes from the tip of the ear through the shoulder, hip, and knee. Usually the dancer will perform the hinge in a standing position with knees bent and heels off the floor. However, the hinge can also be performed on the knees. In any hinge position, it is essential that the body line is diagonally straight and there is no pressure on the lower back.

Jazz Split

A *jazz split* is a half-split position on the floor, in which the front leg is straight and the rear leg is bent as in *attitude*. The jazz split is often reached from a standing position. From a wide fourth position in turnout, the front leg slides forward, while the rear leg bends, remaining as turned out as possible. The torso leans slightly to the side of the forward leg. The arm on the same side as the forward leg reaches to the floor to support the body weight and protect the knee as the dancer slides to the half-split position.

Correct   Incorrect

Lateral

The *lateral* position is any bend to the side. The bend can initiate from the waist or can be merely a tilt of the head and shoulders to the side. The body should not lean forward or backward when executing this position but must bend directly to the side.

Lunge

A *lunge* is a movement in which one foot is advanced as far as possible with the knee bent and directly over the instep while the other foot remains stationary. The legs are either in parallel or turned-out second or fourth position, with one leg bent and one leg straight. Torso position can vary; however, the center of weight will always be closer to the bent leg.

STANDING STRETCHES

These exercises are mainly used as a means to warm up the body. They are initially performed at a slow pace, with a gradual increase in speed as the body gets warmer. By performing standing exercises before sitting exercises, the body is allowed to get an overall warm-up before executing the more demanding floor stretches. The order of standing to floor exercises is not absolute; some teachers prefer the opposite order. In either case, take it easy when you first begin.

Lunge with Opposition Stretch

This torso stretch can be performed in any of the foot positions. As the right arm reaches up toward the ceiling, the right knee bends. Body weight remains centered over both legs, causing the left hip to lift. The stretch is then performed on the opposite side of the body.

Second Position Parallel Forward Stretch

Standing in second position parallel, bend over to bring the hands as close to the floor as possible while keeping the knees straight.

Second Position Parallel Forward Stretch/ Bent Knees

Standing in second position parallel, bend the knees and reach the hands through the legs as far as possible. Slowly straighten the legs and roll the torso up to a vertical position.

Side Stretch

This stretch is usually performed in second position turned out. With the arms extended vertically, reach as far to the side as possible by stretching the waist and rib cage while keeping the back straight.

First Position Parallel Forward Stretch

Standing in parallel first position and keeping the knees straight, bend over to place the hands on the floor. Keeping the hands on the floor, fully bend the knees, allowing the heels to release from the floor. Try to lift the heels as high off the floor as possible and stretch the feet in this position. Next, keeping the hands on the floor, return the heels to the floor and straighten the legs.

Body Wave or Roll

A *body wave* or *roll* is a sequential movement of the torso that can easily be learned from the flat-back position. The movement starts at the lower back with a contraction of the torso and then moves sequentially through the spine. The chin rests on the chest until the wave reaches the neck. The head then falls back, with the chin facing the ceiling. The wave then reverses direction through the torso and head. The body wave is usually a smooth movement and is performed to achieve spinal flexibility.

Back (Released) Stretch

The *back stretch* is usually performed in a parallel first or second position. Place the hands on the hip bones, elbows pressed forward. Slightly bend the knees, tightening the buttocks, arching the upper back, and lifting the chin. This exercise is performed to stretch the chest and strengthen the upper back.

Hand Walk

This exercise stretches the hamstring muscles at the back of the thigh and the Achilles tendon, which runs from the heel to the back calf muscles. From first position parallel, hands on the floor, walk the hands as far away from the feet as possible, keeping the heels in contact with the floor. Attempt to keep the back flat during the hand walk. Hold the stretch and then walk the hands back toward the feet.

Runner Lunges

This stretch is specifically for the Achilles tendon and the muscles of the thigh and hip joint. From a fourth position parallel lunge, place the hands on the floor on either side of the forward bent knee. In this position, the heel of the front foot must remain on the floor. The back leg should be straight, foot fully flexed, with the toes pressed against the floor. Keeping the hands on the floor, straighten the front leg while pressing the heel of the back foot to the floor. Attempt to keep the back flat, pressing the chest toward the front knee. For additional stretch, flex the foot of the front leg, lifting the toes off the floor. Return to the lunge position and repeat the stretch sequence on the opposite leg.

SITTING STRETCHES

The stretches presented on the floor should never be performed without prior warm-up. It is essential to get the body very warm in order to get the maximum benefit from these excellent stretches.

First Position Parallel Stretch

This exercise stretches the hamstring muscles at the back of the thigh. In a straight-back sitting position, with the legs extended forward, grasp the ankles, gently pulling the chest to the thighs. This forward stretch may be performed with the back rounded or flat and the toes pointed or flexed.

Soles-of-the-Feet-Together Stretch

Sitting with the soles of the feet together and the knees bent, hold the ankles and stretch gently forward. This stretch may be done with the back rounded, attempting to press the chest forward toward the floor. The stretch may also be done with the back flat, pressing the pelvic girdle forward. In any of the spinal positions, a more flexible dancer may use the pressure of the lower arm and elbow against the knee to gently push the knees toward the floor to increase the flexibility of the hip joints.

Second Position Straddle Stretch

Sitting with the back straight, open the legs as wide as possible to second position. Several stretches may be performed from this position; all are excellent for increasing hip joint and leg flexibility.

Forward Stretch. Holding the legs in turnout, press the chest forward toward the floor. This stretch may be done with the back rounded or flat and the toes pointed or flexed. Arm position may vary.

Side Stretch. Place the right arm from the elbow to the palm on the floor, either inside or outside the right leg. The left arm reaches overhead while stretching from the waist toward the right leg. The back is held straight, and both hips are solidly placed on the floor. Reverse the entire stretch toward the left leg.

Toward-the-Leg Stretch. Twist from the waist as far as possible toward the right leg. Reach toward the right ankle with both hands, gently pulling the chest toward the right leg. The left hip should remain in contact with the floor. This stretch may be done with the back rounded or flat, and the toes pointed or flexed. Repeat the stretch toward the left leg.

Jazz Split Stretch

Start on the floor in the jazz split position. Reach toward the front leg with both hands and try to touch the chest to the knee. Make sure the rear bent leg is as close to the body as possible so that the knee will not be injured.

From the above position, sweep the arms and body toward the front leg, continuing around to the rear until the back is against the floor. Relax in this position. Make sure the lower back is on the floor even if the bent knee lifts off the floor. This position creates an excellent stretch for the front of the thigh. Recover to the jazz split position by reversing the sweep of the arms and body toward the front leg.

The Plow

The *plow* is derived from yoga. Lying on the back, lift the legs ninety degrees vertically. Continue to lift the legs and the hips off the floor, rolling backward to place the knees bent on the floor next to the ears. Hand support of the lower back may be used at the hips if the position is awkward because of a lack of flexibility in the lower back.

The Plow/Straight Legs

From the bent-knee position, extend the legs with the feet flexed, toes pressed against the floor. As flexibility increases, attempt to lift the hips higher off the floor, continuing to keep the legs straight, feet flexed, and toes pressed against the floor.

The Plow/Pike Stretch

From the plow position/straight legs, point the feet. Grasp the ankles and gently pull the legs toward the chest, attempting to pike (compress) the body as tightly as possible. In the pike position, roll down until the lower back touches the floor and then release the ankles, bend the knees to the chest, and stretch the legs out along the floor.

Cobra Stretch/Upper Back Arch

Cobra is another position derived from yoga. Lying flat on the floor, on the stomach, place the palms on the floor, next to the shoulders. Straighten the arms while arching the upper back. Lift the chin and look toward the ceiling. The hip bones should remain in contact with the floor. Slowly bend the arms to roll the chest down to the starting position.

BODY ISOLATIONS

Body isolations are the trademark of jazz dance, and the student should master them early in training. A body isolation is the movement of only one part of the body. Isolations generally take place at the head, shoulders, ribs, and hips, and are performed in all directions specific to each body part.

The Head

Head isolations are performed by turning the head to the right, left, chin down, chin up, laterally from shoulder to shoulder, and by extending the head forward and backward. The head can also rotate in a complete circle. Looseness in the neck is essential for head isolations.

The Shoulders

The shoulders can elevate, depress, rotate forward and backward, and make a complete circle. The shoulders can isolate to move one shoulder at a time, both in the same direction, or shoulders in opposite directions.

The Ribs

The ribs are probably the hardest part of the body to isolate because in our daily life these movements are rarely executed. The ribs can shift from side to side and can push forward and backward. The ribs can also rotate in a circle. Isolations of the ribs are easier to discover in a sitting position because the hips are stabilized.

The Hips

The hips, like the ribs, move side to side, forward and backward, and in a complete circle. It is easier to move the hips in *plié* because it allows the ligaments of the hips to loosen.

The technique to remember when performing isolation movements is to do just that—isolate. Pay special attention to keeping the shoulders still when moving the neck and keeping the hips still when moving the ribs. The mastery of these simple isolations will lead to *polycentrics*, or the combining of isolated parts. For example, the head will move in one direction while the shoulders isolate in another direction, the hips will circle, and the hands will be creating a flashy, explosive pattern in space!

LOCOMOTOR MOVEMENTS

The term *locomotor* includes any movement of the entire body through a direction in space.

Jazz Walks

There are many varieties of *jazz walks*. They can be performed in *plié*, in *relevé*, with isolation movements, in any direction, and at any tempo. The technique for the basic jazz or dance walk is to roll through the ball of the foot and then lower the heel to the floor. The legs stretch and reach as far as possible, and at least one foot maintains contact with the floor at all times. The jazz walk is stylized with a step longer than the natural stride.

Chassé

Chassé ("chase") is a term borrowed from ballet, where it is defined as a slide. In jazz it is also a sliding movement, but on closer examination, it can be analyzed as a step-together-step. It is a movement that travels forward, backward, or sideward. When performed to its fullest, it brings the dancer into the air. When in the air, the legs should be straight, feet pointed and crossed together in a tight fifth position.

Pas de Bourrée

The *pas de bourrée* ("*bourrée* step," from a seventeenth-century French dance) is a ballet step consisting of a series of three steps. The jazz *pas de bourrée* can be performed in several ways.

Pas de Bourrée in Place, Traveling Forward or Backward. *Pas de bourrée* in place, traveling forward or backward, begins in second position. The first step crosses in front or back. In the second step, the opposite foot steps to second position. In the third step, the first foot steps in place. This *pas de bourrée* may be referred to as "cross, side, front."

Pas de Bourrée Traveling Sideward. In *pas de bourrée* traveling sideward, the first step crosses in back. The second step travels to second position. The third step crosses over the second step, traveling further sideward. This *pas de bourrée* may be referred to as "back, side, front."

Pas de Bourrée Turning. Another *pas de bourrée* is a turning *pas de bourrée*. As in the *pas de bourrée* traveling sideward, the first step crosses in back. The second step turns the body halfway around by stepping toward the back. The third step completes the turn by crossing in front of the second step.

Triplet

A triplet is a three-step movement, with the first step in *plié* and the second and third steps in *relevé*. It usually travels forward, but can also travel backward, to the side, or turning. It can be counted in measures of three's or as *one and two*.

Jazz Slide

The *jazz slide* is initiated by stepping to a turned-out second position lunge and sliding the straight leg along the floor, foot pointed. The hip of the bent leg is pushed in the direction of the lunge so that the body is tilted and asymmetrical. The arms are in second position but, because the body is tilted, they are on an oblique line parallel to the extended sliding leg.

Jazz Square

The *jazz square* consists of four walking steps performed in a square. The first step travels forward, the second crosses in front of the first, the third step travels backward, and the fourth step opens to the side. The hips and arms are usually used in this step to stylize and accent the movements.

Hitch Kick

In the *hitch kick*, the legs pass each other in a scissorlike fashion in the air; thus the first kicking leg becomes the landing support leg.

Hitch Kick Forward. The *hitch kick forward* begins with a lunge forward to a *demi-plié.* The rear leg is then kicked forward. As the body rises in the air, the legs pass in scissorlike fashion as the second leg is also kicked forward. The landing is on the first kicking leg in a *demi-plié,* with the second kicking leg still held high. The kicking legs are held straight throughout.

The hitch kick forward may also be done from the lunge with the first kicking leg bent and the second kicking leg straight.

Hitch Kick to the Rear. The *hitch kick to the rear* begins with a lunge onto one leg in *demi-plié*. The rear leg is then kicked backward. As the body rises in the air, the legs pass in scissorlike fashion as the second leg is also kicked backward. The landing is on the first kicking leg in a *demi-plié*, with the second kicking leg held high in an *arabesque*. The kicking legs are held straight throughout.

Hitch Kick to the Side. The *hitch kick to the side* begins with a sideward lunge into a *demi-plié*. The trailing leg follows with a straight kick to the side in the direction of movement, crossing over the bent leg. As the body rises in the air, the legs pass in scissorlike fashion as the second leg opens in a straight kick to the side. The landing is on the first kicking leg, quickly followed by the second kicking leg to end in fourth position *demi-plié*.

Fan Kick

In the *fan kick*, the leg makes a sweeping arc through space. It crosses in front of the body, then sweeps to make a half circle before touching the ground. The sweeping leg can be either straight or in *attitude*; ideally the leg should be at hip level. The supporting leg can be in *plié*, *relevé*, or *relevé* with a bent knee (termed *plié-relevé*).

Kick-Ball Change

The *kick-ball* change is a step derived from tap dance. This step is counted *one and two* and is regularly used as a transition step because it involves little or no traveling. One leg kicks as high as determined by flexibility or choreography. The kicking leg steps to the rear of the supporting leg, placing the weight on the ball of the foot, heel lifted. The other foot then steps in place with the weight changing or transfering onto this foot; hence the name kick-ball change.

OPPOSITIONAL MOVES

Most locomotor movements use the arms in some way. The arms and legs are often coordinated in opposition. *Opposition* means that the opposite arm and leg are forward during a step; for example, in the *chassé*, the right foot steps out on the first step and the left arm extends forward. The same is true for jazz walks; when the left foot steps forward, the right arm will be forward. In a fan kick with the right leg, often the left arm will sweep overhead in the opposite direction. The term *opposition* is used for other body parts as well; for example, in isolations, the right shoulder and left hip may lift simultaneously.

TURNS

Turns are rotating movements performed in place or traveling. They are executed by turning the whole body on two feet, one foot, from one foot to the other, or while jumping. Remember that the secret to successful turns is *spotting* (see page 43).

Paddle Turn

The *paddle turn* is a simple turn that pivots the body around one spot. The weight is continually shifted from one foot to the other. The supporting stationary leg pivots on the ball of the foot, with the heel lifting slightly off the floor. The other leg is extended to the side and "paddles" on the ball of the foot, rotating the body in a circular direction while the foot traces an imaginary circular pattern on the floor.

Pivot Turn

A *pivot turn* is performed on two feet. The pivot is generally performed on the balls of the feet, quickly changing the direction of the body to face the opposite direction. Both feet remain on the floor in their positions when the body is pivoted.

Chaîné Turn

Chaîné ("chained") turns derive from ballet but are also included in jazz dance. A *chaîné* turn is a two-step turn generally performed in *relevé*, but it may also be performed in *plié*. The body rotates 180 degrees on each step of the turn, and the turning movement progresses in a straight line. The weight shifts from one leg to the other with evenly balanced steps. In *chaîné* turns performed in *relevé*, legs should be held in first position turned out. In *chaîné* turns performed in *plié*, the legs may be held parallel or turned out in either first or second position.

Piqué Turn

The *piqué* ("point") turn is another turn borrowed from ballet. It is a full turn performed turned out in *relevé* on one foot and progresses in a straight line. Prepare for the turn with one leg in *demi-plié* and the other leg straight forward. Begin the turn by stepping sideward with the straight leg onto the half-toe (*relevé*). The opposite leg closes to a low *passé* position behind the knee of the straight leg during the turn. The turn ends in the preparation position, and the straight leg then steps sideward again to execute the next turn. It is important to extend the leg fully when stepping onto the half-toe and to step directly under the straight leg when coming to *plié* from the *passé* position.

Pirouette

The *pirouette* ("whirling about") is a ballet turn performed in place, with one leg in *relevé* and the other in *passé*. The *pirouette* may be performed in parallel or turned out position. Parallel *pirouettes* may also be done with the supporting leg in *plié*. In performing *pirouettes*, bring the lifted knee directly to high *passé*, maintain good alignment, and spot.

Soutenu Turn

The *soutenu* ("sustained") turn also originates in ballet. In jazz, the *soutenu* turn may rotate in quarter turns, half turns, or whole turns. Prepare for the turn by stepping to parallel second in *plié*, pulling the second leg in to meet the preparation leg as the turn is executed with both legs in *relevé*. The weight of the body is shared equally by both legs during the turn. The turn may be executed either inward or outward, with the second leg being pulled in to cross either in front or in back of the preparation leg.

JUMPS

Jump refers to any aerial (unsupported) movement. Jumps can be performed traveling forward, sideward, backward, or turning. The movement principles outlined on page 43 should be followed in all jumps. The five kinds of jazz dance jumps are defined below.

Jump

A *jump* is an aerial movement that takes off from two feet and lands on two feet. Variations are defined by the shape of the legs. Jumps can be performed with one or both legs straight or bent, with the legs split in the air, or with quarter, half, or whole turns.

Hop

A *hop* is an aerial movement that takes off on one foot and lands on that same foot. Variations exist as they do with jumps. A popular jazz hop is the *passé* hop, with the lifted leg in high *passé*.

Assemblé

Assemblé is a ballet term meaning "assembled." It is any aerial movement that starts on either one foot or both feet and ends with both feet together.

Sissonne

The *sissonne* (named for the originator of the step) is a ballet jump that takes off from both feet and lands on one foot, with the other leg lifted in the air. The lifted leg may end in any position desired: *attitude* side, front, or back; *battement* front or side; *arabesque;* or *passé.*

Leap/Jeté

The *jeté* is the grandest jump. It is a large jump from one foot to the other, the legs creating the vision of an arc in the air. Usually the legs are spread wide apart; however, the *jeté* may be done in a variety of leg positions—splits, *attitudes*, or stags (one leg bent and one leg straight).

Chapter 6

Putting It All Together

Dance is comprised of more than just dance steps. The dancer also communicates time, space, and dynamics. By understanding how to work with these three dance elements, a dancer can create an entire dance made up solely of walking, running, or other simple movements. It is the variation of time, space, and dynamics that gives life to the dance and energy to the dancer and that can turn a movement into an artistic expression. The dancer's ability to project these elements as well as inner feelings that relate to the movement is also essential for an exciting performance. In this chapter, we discuss the basic elements inherent to all dance

Radio City Music Hall. These dancers radiate with stage projection. Photo by Martha Swope.

and how to acquire the confidence and ability to project the total dance experience. We have also included simple dance combinations that will help the student to put all these ideas together.

TIME: FIND THE BEAT AND COUNT IT

As colors create a mood in painting, music sets the mood in dance. Music also provides the rhythmic structure underlying all dance movements. The dancer must be able to count the beat, recognize the accents, and hear the rhythmic patterns and musical phrasing. These skills will enable you as a dancer to respond quickly and precisely to the music.

Beat

The *beat* is the basic unit of musical time. The *beat* can be heard as a regular pulsation underlying the music, similar to the ticking of a clock.

Tempo

The *tempo* of a piece of music is the speed at which it is performed. A number of Italian terms are used to indicate the tempo of a piece. Listed from the slowest to the fastest, they are

Largo	very slow, broad
Lento	slow
Adagio	slow ("at ease")
Andante	moderate ("walking")
Moderato	moderate
Allegretto	fast
Allegro	fast ("cheerful")
Presto	very fast
Prestissimo	as fast as possible

Meter and Measure

Written music is divided into groups of notes called *measures* (also known as *bars*), each having a specific number of beats. *Meter* is the basic number of beats per measure.

Time Signature

The meter of a piece of music is indicated by a *time signature* at the beginning of the piece. The time signature is written as two numbers, one above the other. The top number indicates the number of beats per measure; the bottom number indicates the kind of note (half note, quarter note, etc.) that receives one beat. The common waltz time signature of 3/4 indicates that there are three beats to the measure and that a quarter note receives one beat.

Note Values

Written music shows not only which note should be played, but the relative duration of one note to another through a system of *note values*. At the top of the note-value tree shown in Figure 6-1 is a whole note. Each of the lines below it is equal in duration to a whole note. Two half notes equal a whole note, as do four quarter notes, eight eighth notes, and sixteen sixteenth notes. It should be understood that these note values are relative to each other, rather than absolute, since the time allotted the notes depends on the tempo of the piece.

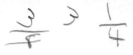

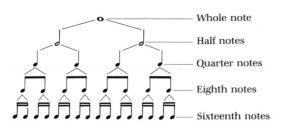

Figure 6-1 Note-Value Tree

Simple Meter

Simple meters have two, three, or four beats per measure. Examples of simple meter are

2/2, 2/4, 2/8   two beats per measure

3/2, 3/4, 3/8   three beats per measure

4/2, 4/4, 4/8   four beats per measure

In jazz music, simple meters are sometimes combined to form *irregular meters*, such as 5/4—a combination of the simple meters 2/4 and 3/4. Unusual meters such as 5/4 and 7/4 are frequently used by such jazz composers as Dave Brubeck and Bill Evans.

Compound Meter

Compound meters are simple meters multiplied by three. Examples of compound meter are

6/2, 6/4, 6/8   six (3 × 2) beats per measure

9/4, 9/8   nine (3 × 3) beats per measure

12/4, 12/8   twelve (3 × 4) beats per measure

Mixed Meter

In *mixed meter*, the time signature may change several times within a single piece of music. Examples of mixed meter may be found in many Beatles songs:

"Good Day Sunshine"   4/4, 3/4

"All You Need Is Love"   4/4, 3/4, 4/4, 3/4, 4/4, 2/4

"Strawberry Fields Forever"   4/4, 2/4, 4/4, 2/4, 6/8, 9/8, 4/4

"Blackbird"   3/4, 4/4, 6/4, 4/4, 6/4, 3/4

Accent and Syncopation

Accent is emphasis on one note or chord. In simple meter, the accent is generally on the *downbeat*—the first beat of the measure. *Syncopation* places the accent on normally unaccented beats of the measure. The three most common means of syncopation are (1) holding a note on the first beat for the length of two beats; (2) skipping the first beat altogether and replacing it with a silence (a *rest*); and (3) accenting normally weak beats, such as the *upbeat*—the last beat of the measure. Another means of syncopation, common to jazz music, is to create a hesitation by playing a note slightly sooner or later than it would normally be played. Syncopation, a trademark of jazz, adds to the surprise and spontaneity of jazz dance.

Rhythmic Pattern

Rhythmic pattern is created by the combination of note values, accents, and meter. For example,

A simple waltz in 3/4 time with the accent on the first beat of the measure would have a rhythmic pattern of **one**-two-three, **one**-two-three, **one**-two-three.

A typical march in 2/4 time with the accent on the first beat would have a rhythmic pattern of **one**-two, **one**-two, **one**-two.

Normally accented 4/4 time would have a rhythmic pattern of **one**-two-*three*-four, **one**-two-*three*-four, with the major accent on the first beat and a lesser accent on the third beat.

A syncopated rhythm in 4/4 time might have a rhythmic pattern of one-**and**-two-**and**-three-**and**-four-**and,** one-**and**-two-**and**-three-**and**-four-**and;** or, accenting the upbeat, one-two-three-**four,** one-two-three-**four,** one-two-three-**four.**

More-complicated rhythmic patterns are created as notes of differing values (quarter note, eighth note, sixteenth note, etc.) are combined (see Figure 6-2).

Musical Phrases

A *musical phrase* is a division of the musical line, somewhat comparable to a clause or a sentence in prose. Although it may take some practice for you to recognize musical phrases, it will be helpful to think of them as short musical statements that come to recognizable points of arrival—points where a singer might take a breath.

A musical phrase is at least two measures long. Generally in jazz dance classes, music in 4/4 time is counted in two-measure phrases totaling eight counts. Breaking the sequence of a dance combination into phrases of eight counts makes it easier for the dancer to remember the steps. When counting and keeping track of the phrases, the teacher

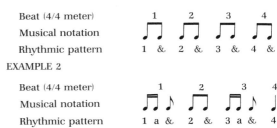

Figure 6-2 Complicated Rhythmic Patterns

will very often number them by counting *1*-2-3-4-5-6-7-8, 2-2-3-4-5-6-7-8, 3-2-3-4-5-6-7-8, etc.

An understanding of basic musical terms is essential to the beginning dancer. With continued exposure to music, a dancer will develop an ability to recognize tempos, meters, accents, rhythmic patterns, and musical phrases.

Exercises for the Study of Time

Exercise 1. Using either a drum or recorded music, perform a simple movement, such as a jazz walk, across the floor. Move four counts on the beat: 1-2-3-4. Next, move four counts off the beat: 1-**and**-2-**and**-3-**and**-4-**and.** Alternate every four counts, first moving on the beat, then off the beat.

Exercise 2. Listen to music with 4/4 meter and identify its accent. Once the accent is identified, move only on the accented beats, holding the movement during the unaccented beats. Repeat this exercise with 2/4 and 3/4 meter.

Exercise 3. Perform a simple locomotor movement, such as a walk or run, for an entire musical phrase. When a new phrase begins, perform a new locomotor movement. Continue this exercise through an entire piece of music.

Exercise 4. Practice clapping the following rhythmic patterns and then choreograph movements that respond to these patterns:

a. 1 a & 2   3   & 4
b. 1   & 2 a & 3   4 a &
c. 1   2   3 a & 4   &
d. 1 a & 2   & 3

SPACE

In addition to an awareness of the element of time—the *when* in dance: when to move, step, gesture, turn, and jump—the dancer must also develop a sensitivity to *space.*

Awareness of space is the knowledge of *where:* where the dancer must go in relationship both to the other dancers in the space and to the audience. The dancer's space is affected by the direction the movement takes, the two-dimensional pattern created by the movement, the level of the movement, and its dimension or size.

Direction

Primary movement directions are forward, backward, sideward, diagonal, and circular. These directions can also be defined in conventional stage

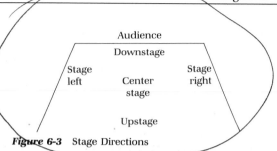

Figure 6-3 Stage Directions

terminology, which describes their relationship to the audience (see Figure 6-3). *Downstage* is the part of the stage closest to the audience. *Upstage* is the part of the stage farthest from the audience. *Stage left* is to the performer's left while facing the audience. *Stage right* is to the performer's right while facing the audience.

Spatial direction can also refer to directional adjustments of isolated body movements, such as a turn of the head, a raise of the arm, or a bend of the torso.

Spatial Pattern

The spatial pattern is the two-dimensional path a dancer follows. The spatial pattern is affected by the dance steps and the dancer's position in relation to other dancers on the stage and to the audience; the more dancers onstage, the more intricate the patterns can become. Primary spatial patterns are the square, circle, rectangle, triangle, zigzag, and figure eight.

Level

Level changes are determined by the positions the body assumes and by the height of the dancer in the space. Level changes create variety within the individual dancer's movements. Primary movement levels are lying, sitting, kneeling, standing, and jumping. Exciting level changes can occur with the use of varied jumps and falls.

Dimension

Dimension refers to the size of a dance movement and the space occupied by the body. The dimension of a movement can be altered in length, depth, or breadth. For example, a walk may be performed with big or small steps, thereby altering its length and affecting the amount of space the body occupies. The dimension of a movement is often affected by the other dancers occupying the space. When all dancers are performing the same movement, they must execute it with the same dimension or else they may find they have infringed upon another's space.

Exercises for the Study of Space

Exercise 1: Direction. Select a locomotor movement. Perform the movement traveling in all the primary directions: forward, backward, sideward, diagonal, and circular.

Exercise 2: Spatial Pattern. Select a simple locomotor combination. Perform the combination in the primary spatial patterns: square, circle, rectangle, triangle, zigzag, and figure eight.

Exercise 3: Level. Perform a simple upper body movement. Repeat it lying, sitting, kneeling, standing, and jumping.

Exercise 4: Dimension. Select a simple eight-count dance combination. Perform the movements as large as possible. Perform the movements as small as possible.

DYNAMICS

Dynamics refers to how a movement is performed: the intensity of its energy and the dynamic qualities of its performance. The same movement will appear different, depending on the intensity of the energy used for its performance. For example, raising an arm as if it were light as a feather would take minimal energy, whereas raising an arm as if it were a heavy log would take greater energy. Both the appearance and performance of these two moves would be different. It is the intensity of the energy output that creates the variety.

The following terms are commonly used to describe dynamic qualities in jazz dance. These qualities are affected by the intensity of energy with which the movement is performed.

Percussive movement has a sharp, striking quality. There is a sharp, forceful initiation of movement and a definite cessation of movement. A percussive movement often appears as an accent because it is a sudden use of energy. This accent may be strong or slight, depending on the intensity of energy. A stomp, clap, snap, and punch are examples of accented or percussive movements.

Sustained movement has a prolonged quality and seems to have no beginning or end. Sustained movement is smooth, restrained, continuous, and unaccented. A slow, controlled lift of the arm is an example of a sustained movement.

Vibratory movement has a shaking or trembling effect. Vibratory movements may be very fast, recurring percussive movements, which in jazz dance may be performed in isolated body parts. A shoulder shimmy is an example of vibratory movement.

Suspension of a movement is the period of time during which the motion of a movement is lifted and held—the brief moment before the body succumbs to the pull of gravity. Suspended movement has a quality of weightlessness or breathlessness; it is often observed in a leap at the moment when the dancer appears suspended in air. It is also a hold in any movement before its completion.

A *swing* is akin to a pendulum movement. The speed of a swing increases at the bottom of its path and slows as the swing rises. Before the repetition of the pendulum swing, there seems to be a momentary pause, which has the quality of a release of body tension.

A *collapse* is the total release of body tension and the succumbing to the pull of gravity. The collapse is often followed by a recovery movement.

Exercises for the Study of Dynamics

Exercise 1. Select a simple movement combination. Perform the combination three times, each time using a different energy level:

a. As little energy as possible
b. A maximum amount of energy
c. A varied energy level

Exercise 2. Select a simple movement combination. Perform the combination six times, each time using a different dynamic quality:

a. Percussive movement
b. Sustained movement
c. Vibratory movement
d. Suspension
e. Swing
f. Collapse

PROJECTION

Much has been discussed regarding the technical aspects of dance and the control of temporal, spatial, and dynamic elements. Although the beginning dancer must spend countless hours learning the basic skills of dance and the various qualities of dance movement, the idea of projection must also be explored before the dancer can fully appreciate the joy of dancing.

Projection is the communication of a vivid image to the audience through attitude, eye contact, facial expression, and full body commitment to the dance movements. A dancer who projects well is able to easily communicate the elements of time, space, and dynamics. In fact, without this full commitment to the dance, the artistic expression is lost within the dancer. By developing the ability to *project*, the dancer can strongly affect the audience and gain a sense of self-fulfillment from having given an emotionally moving performance.

For beginning students, the development of projection can be a creative and self-actualizing process. It is a challenge to perform the dance movements accurately and yet be free to expand one's focus beyond oneself. At all times the dancer should be continually aware of the importance of projection, whether it be to an audience, other students in class, the teacher, or only the image in the mirror. The ability to project one's inner feelings comes with confidence in one's technical ability.

When that confidence becomes habitual, the dancer's individual style becomes apparent and the performance becomes unique and truly exciting.

BASIC COMBINATIONS FOR HOME AND CLASS STUDY

Outlined below are basic combinations that can be used for practice at home as well as in the classroom. The student and teacher are encouraged to manipulate these combinations by changing their tempos, directions, dimensions, and dynamics. See how many other combinations can be built from the basic ones below. For a review of the steps and movements listed in these combinations, see Chapter 5, "Basic Jazz Dance."

Combination 1

Counts	
1	Jazz walk left
2	Jazz walk right
3	Jazz walk left
4&-5	*Pas de bourrée* right
6&-7	*Pas de bourrée* left
8	*Pirouette* turning right, with right foot in parallel *passé*

Combination 2

Counts	
1	Jazz walk right
2	Jazz walk left
3	Jazz walk right
4	Jazz walk left
5	Step right
6	Half pivot turn
7	Step right
8	Half pivot turn

Combination 3

Counts	
1&-2	*Chassé* right
3&-4	*Chassé* left
5-6-7-8	Jazz square right
1-2	Fan kick right
3-4	Fan kick left
5-6-7-8	Jazz square right

Combination 4

Counts	
1	*Relevé* walk right
2	*Relevé* walk left
3	*Plié* walk right
4	*Plié* walk left
5 & 6	*Chaîné* turn right
7 & 8	*Chaîné* turn left
1	*Relevé* walk right
2	*Relevé* walk left
3	*Plié* walk right
4	*Plié* walk left
5-6-7-8	Jazz slide facing front

Combination 5

Counts	
1-2	Step right, hop with left foot in parallel *passé*
3-4	Step left, hop with right foot in parallel *passé*
5-6-7-8	Four jazz walks in a circle: right, left, right, left
1&-2	Kick-ball change with right kick
3	Step right
4	Step left into fourth position *plié* (preparation)
5	*Pirouette* from fourth position, turning right, with right foot in *passé*

6	Step on right foot in *plié*
7	Touch left foot side
8	Jump, feet together (parallel first position) and clap hands together

Combination 6

Counts

1&-2	*Pas de bourrée* right
3&-4	*Pas de bourrée* left
5-6	Hitch kicks in two counts, kicking right, then left, landing on right
7	Step left
8	Leap right

After practicing the above sequences, improvise by incorporating turns, falls, and jumps into the combinations. Isolations can be included in the sequences. For example, in combination 2, the jazz walks may be performed with hip or shoulder isolations to add interest to the basic walk.

Chapter 7

The Dancer's Instrument: Taking Care of It

Although dance is considered an art form, it is also a demanding physical activity. Every dancer should know the essentials of body maintenance, including preparing the body for activity, preventing and caring for injuries, and establishing proper nutritional habits.

PRE–WARM-UP EXERCISES

A warm-up is like tuning a fine instrument. The body must also be prepared to respond to the demands placed upon it. Often a jazz dance class will

Ann Reinking in Dancin' *by Bob Fosse. The dancer's instrument is the body; thus the dancer must know how to take excellent care of it. Photo by Martha Swope.*

begin with fairly vigorous exercises. The result of inadequate warm-up may be such injuries as torn or pulled muscles, sprains, cramps, and spasms.

The dancer should allow approximately ten minutes before class for an individual pre–warm-up. The purpose of the pre–warm-up is to increase body heat through light to moderate exercise. Extra attention should be paid to warming up any area of the body that is weak or prone to injury.

Floor Exercises for the Ankle, Knee, and Hip Joints

The pre–warm-up may begin in any position. However, it is good to begin by lying on the floor to relieve the body of the additional stress of working against the pull of gravity, so that full attention can be paid to maintaining proper body placement. The following simple exercises may be used in warming up the ankle, knee, and hip joints.

Exercise 1.   Lying flat on the back, flex and point the toes, moving only the toes and metatarsal arch (do not move the ankle joint). Repeat eight times with each foot.

Exercise 2.   Lying flat on the back, flex and extend the foot at the ankle. Repeat eight times with each foot.

Exercise 3.   Lying flat on the back, rotate the ankles in both directions. Repeat eight times with each foot.

Exercise 4.   Knee to chest: Lying flat on the back with the knees bent and the soles of the feet flat on the ground, raise one knee toward the chest. Return to the starting position and repeat with the opposite knee. Repeat four times on each side.

Exercise 5.   Knee to chest in turnout position: Begin as in exercise 4, rotating the knee to the side when the knee is at the chest. Rotate the knee in again and return to the starting position. Repeat four times on each side.

Exercise 6. Lower-back twist: Lying flat on the back, extend arms straight out to the side, palms down on the floor. Lift one knee toward the chest. Twisting the lower back, lower the knee to the floor by the opposite arm. Relax in this position. Lift the knee back to the chest and lower the leg to the floor. Repeat four times on each side.

While still on the floor; the student should also perform the alignment exercises outlined on pages 30—33.

Standing Exercises for the Upper Torso and Weight-Bearing Joints

Once the student has completed a floor pre–warm-up, additional standing exercises can be used to warm up the upper torso and weight-bearing joints.

Exercise 1. Neck circles: Repeat four times to the right, four times to the left.

Exercise 2. Arm circles: Repeat four times forward, four times backward.

Exercise 3. Waist twists: Twist side to side a total of eight times.

Exercise 4. Foot roll and prance: Stand with feet in parallel first position. Bend one knee, rolling through the ball of the foot to the pointed toe. Finally, lift the tip of the toe a few inches above the floor. Return the foot to the floor, reversing the action of the foot. Repeat several times at a slow tempo. Do the exercise at a quicker tempo, springing the foot off the floor. Repeat with the opposite foot.

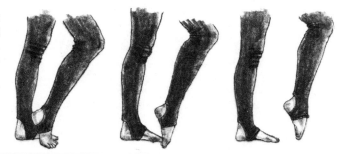

Exercise 5. Knee swing-out: This exercise may be done using the barre for support or in center floor. Stand with the feet turned out. Lift the knee to the side, then swing across the body in front of the supporting leg. Reverse the swing, returning the leg to the side-lift position. Repeat several swings on each leg. This exercise will help warm up the front and inner thigh muscles and the hip joints.

INJURIES

In most situations, if the student works in proper alignment, is adequately warmed up, and uses correct dance technique, injury is unlikely to occur.

Muscle Soreness

Usually the most common ailment of the beginning dancer is muscle soreness. The best way to relieve this discomfort is to exercise the body again as soon as possible. The dancer may also want to take a hot bath or shower to relieve the temporary soreness. There are, however, certain injuries common to dancers that are more serious and require proper first-aid treatment to prevent possible permanent damage.

I-C-E: The Magic Word

In the event of injury, a simple way to remember first-aid treatment is by keeping in mind the initials **I-C-E.**

I   Ice: Apply ice immediately for eight to ten minutes at a time, allowing the injured body part to regain its normal body temperature between icings.

C   Compression: Wrap the injured body part with an elastic or one-piece bandage while applying ice.

E   Elevation: Raise the injured body part.

Ice, compression, and elevation should be applied immediately after an injury for the first hour. However, depending upon the severity of the injury, the icing first-aid technique may continue for as long as twenty-four hours, icing approximately every two to three hours. The purpose of the ice, compression, and elevation is to reduce the swelling of the body part, allowing faster healing.

Listed below are injuries that may require first-aid treatment. If the injury persists beyond the icing process, with minimal healing, a physician should be consulted.

Cramp

A cramp is a painful, spasmodic muscle contraction and is usually due to overfatigue of a muscle. It may also be caused by a mineral imbalance. To relieve the pain, gently stretch or massage the cramped part. Stomach cramps may result from eating heavily prior to class.

Strain

A strain, or muscle pull, is the overstretching of a muscle, sometimes involving a minute tear of the muscle fibers or adjacent tissues. Most commonly, strains occur in the muscles of the thigh, calf, hip joints, and lower back. A strain should be treated with ice and compression. To prevent further incidence of strains, the dancer should have an understanding of how the injury occurred. Improper warm-up is often a cause of muscle strain.

Sprain

A more serious injury is the sprain, a sudden or violent twisting or wrenching of a joint, causing the stretching or tearing of ligaments and often the rupture of blood vessels with hemorrhage into the surrounding tissues. Symptoms of the sprain include swelling, inflammation, point tenderness, and discoloration. Sprains are most common to the dancer's ankles and knees. Treatment should include immediate icing and compression. Early movement of the joint is also important, but must be of a non-weight-bearing nature. Depending upon the severity of the sprain, medical treatment by a doctor may be advisable.

Shin Splints

Shin splints are characterized by a sharp pain in the muscles along the front and outside of the lower leg (the tibia, or shin bone). This condition may be a result of falling arches, muscle fatigue or stress from overuse, or overdevelopment of the calf muscle. If the calf muscle becomes overdeveloped (a common problem in dancing), the muscles on the front or anterior aspect of the shin bone are stretched and weakened because of the overuse of the stronger calf muscle. This imbalance of muscle strength on the front (anterior) and back (posterior) muscles of the shin bone often results in shin splints for the dancer. Dancing on hard surfaces or improper landing from a jump may also cause shin splints. The most common first-aid treatments for shin splints are icing the legs prior to class, taking aspirin to reduce the inflammation of the tendon surrounding the shin bone, whirlpool baths, shin-splint strapping, and, in severe cases, ultrasound therapy by a physical therapist.

NUTRITION

"I'm too fat" is a common complaint of dancers. Since the dancer is before the mirror the majority of class time, a strong emphasis is put on body image. Dance clothing reveals every bulge and extra pound; thus the dancer must be unusually aware of diet and nutritional habits.

Rather than thinking in terms of "diet," which provokes a negative response from most people, the dancer should try to develop good nutritional habits that can be sustained throughout a lifetime. The old rule of making a balanced selection of foods from the "basic four" food groups still applies.

A nutritionally adequate diet consists of:

1. Milk and milk products
2. Meats, fish, poultry, eggs, and substitutes of nuts, legumes, tofu, and soybean products
3. Fruits and vegetables
4. Breads and cereals

To fully understand the basics of proper nutrition, the dancer should also become familiar with the types of nutrients that the body requires and the functions that each performs.

Protein

The function of protein is to build and repair body tissue. Protein foods are found in groups 1 and 2 of the "basic four" and should constitute approximately 10 or 15 percent of the diet.

Carbohydrates

Carbohydrates are commonly known as sugars and starches. The components of carbohydrates are broken down by the body into a simple sugar called glucose, which is the body's primary source of energy. Carbohydrate foods are found in groups 3 and 4 of the "basic four" and should constitute approximately 50 or 60 percent of the diet.

Fats

Fats have the highest energy content of all nutrients and should make up approximately 30 percent of the diet. Sources of fats include dairy products, fatty meats, margarine, mayonnaise, nuts, seeds, and oils. However, two thirds of fat intake should consist of nonsaturated and polyunsaturated fats, which are found in vegetables and such vegetable oils as corn, cottonseed, safflower, sesame seed, soybean, and sunflower seed oils. The body has a variety of needs for fats: as a reserve fuel supply; for the support and protection of organs; and, finally, as an aid to the utilization of the fat-soluble vitamins A, D, E, and K.

Vitamins and Minerals

Vitamins function in the utilization and absorption of other nutrients and are necessary for the normal metabolic functioning of the body. Vitamins are divided into two groups, based on solubility: Fat-soluble vitamins (A, D, E, and K) tend to remain stored in the body and are usually not excreted in the urine. Water-soluble vitamins (C and B) are excreted in the urine and do not store in the body in appreciable amounts. Minerals are the building materials for tissue and serve as body regulators.

Vitamins and minerals are found in all food groups, especially in unrefined, natural foods. A balanced diet will provide an adequate balance of vitamins and minerals.

Calories

A nutritionally balanced diet will aid the body in its response to the physical demands placed upon it during dance class. The dancer must also make an intelligent evaluation of the body's caloric needs. A dancer cannot afford to take in extra food and calories that do not make a positive contribution to the body.

In evaluating your diet, you should keep an accurate record of foods eaten and the number of calories of each food. The record should show the total amount of calories consumed, with separate categories indicating how many calories were proteins, carbohydrates, and fats. A balanced diet should show from 10 to 15 percent of the calories as proteins, 50 to 60 percent as carbohydrates, and 30 percent as fats. If the record shows an imbalance between categories, a change should be made in eating habits.

In addition to a balanced diet, the dancer needs a balance between total food intake and exercise output. If total food intake and exercise output are consistently balanced, weight will be maintained. If the dancer wishes to lose weight, calorie intake must be less than the number of calories burned by the body in activity.

Calories should not be eliminated totally from one food group, as in many crash or fad diets. Diets that eliminate weight quickly do not give the body time to adapt to the lower calorie intake, and the body usually gains back the lost weight. In starvation diets, much of the weight loss includes lean body tissue as well as fat. As a result, the dancer loses strength and becomes easily fatigued. Other diets that promote quick weight loss by the elimination of water cause dehydration and the loss of important minerals. Many dancers wear plastic sweat pants in class to lose water weight, but the excessive sweating results in loss of potassium and may cause cramping.

Any weight-loss program should adhere to the rules of sound nutrition. Food should be chosen from the "basic four" food groups, with balanced percentages of proteins, carbohydrates, and fats. Weight reduction will occur if total caloric intake is less than the energy expenditure of the body. A weight-reduction program should also be consistent and evenly paced.

In summary, the body is the dancer's instrument. If it is properly cared for, nutritionally and physically, it will respond to the demands placed upon it in a positive manner, and you as a dancer will receive maximum results for your efforts.

Chapter 8

The Dancer's Next Step

The dancer's next step is a look at jazz dance beyond the basic knowledge of fundamental steps, techniques, and movement combinations. Following an introductory jazz dance course, the student may want to seek additional dance training in a variety of jazz dance styles, experience jazz dance choreography, and have the ultimate experience of performing in a dance production. This chapter deals with these topics.

A Chorus Line, *choreography by Michael Bennett. This musical reveals the truth about dance auditions. Photo by Martha Swope.*

ADDITIONAL TRAINING

With the continued study of jazz dance, the student will recognize the need for additional training in body alignment and dance technique. Jazz dancers may increase their progress by studying ballet in conjunction with jazz dance. Ballet training is extremely beneficial as it focuses on body alignment and the technical analysis of dance steps. Skills learned in ballet class will add clarity to the line and movement of a jazz dancer and will extend the dancer's ability.

Most schools offering jazz dance classes will also have ballet classes. It is essential that the student choose a ballet teacher who concentrates on developing technique. The dancer will benefit most from a teacher who stresses proper body placement, with emphasis on individual variations and corrections. A minimum of two ballet lessons per week is suggested for the jazz dancer.

JAZZ DANCE STYLES

Although technique is the foundation of dance, performance is characterized by *style*. In jazz dance, style is usually a combination of various dance influences. Each performer mentioned in the history of jazz dance acquired fame through uniquely stylized dance movements.

Jazz dance is endless in its variations in style. However, three general styles are current, each style reflecting a different dance influence.

Lyrical Jazz

Lyrical jazz is strongly influenced by ballet. Its movements utilize the entire body, extending the body lines and avoiding sharp, angular movements. An example of lyrical jazz is the Luigi technique. Luigi warm-up and center combinations utilize ballet technique but are performed with asymmetrical body lines, increased and varied movements of the spine, and syncopated rhythms and movements.

Funky/Disco Jazz

Although the funky/disco style of jazz dance may often be referred to as L.A. jazz dance, dance studios in New York and across the country teach it. Compared with lyrical jazz dance, funky/disco jazz dance is angular and disjointed. It requires more hip isolations, shoulder shrugs, and head rolls. Dance movements are more pedestrian, emphasizing walking, hand clapping, finger snapping, and general body isolations. Many of its dance steps come from social dance: the jitterbug, the two step, the frug.

Afro Jazz

Afro jazz stems from African movements explored by Katherine Dunham in the 1940s. The style is primitive, with major attention to movements of the spine, neck, and hips. The legs are usually in *plié*. The basic steps of Afro jazz dance are used repetitively in center combinations. Many of the movements are duplications of movements used in African ceremonies, thus giving a hypnotic and ritualistic feeling to the dance style.

We suggest that you experience each of the basic jazz dance styles. In time, you will be able to distinguish which style or styles best suit your movement abilities.

JAZZ DANCE CHOREOGRAPHY

In many jazz dance courses, the student is given the opportunity to develop a dance combination. Choreographing a dance combination follows certain logical steps: selecting and analyzing the music, developing dance movements to fit the music, and creating patterns of movement according to the dance group size decided upon.

Music Selection

The first decision to be made in choreography is the music to be used. It is vital that the music inspires movement. Listen and move to various music selections.

Music Analysis

Once the music is selected, listen to the piece many times. Count the measures in the music, using eight beats to the measure, since that is the most understandable count for dancers. After the measures are counted, group them into musical phrases. Finally, listen for phrases that are repeated in the music. Make notes on each of the above steps.

Movement Selection

After analyzing the music, attempt various dance movements with the music phrases, trying to introduce jumps, turns, and floor work into appropriate places in the music. Through trial and error you will find movements that seem to coincide with the music.

Improvise a phrase of movement to a phrase of music. Create a new movement phrase when the musical phrase changes. Repeat movement phrases when the musical phrase repeats. Repetitive movement phrases build continuity and restate the theme of the dance. Create accents in dance movements to coincide with musical accents. Movement phrases that complement and contrast with a phrase of music may also be used to add new dimension to the music instead of merely reflecting it.

Make use of your total movement vocabulary. Do not hesitate to create new movements or to use movements performed by other dancers. You can create variation in dance movements by using all the elements of dance: time, space, and dynamics (that is, by performing the movements in different tempos, in different directions, or with different dynamics).

Dance Group Size Selection

In a solo dance performance, emphasis is placed upon the technical and creative aspects of the dance movements. The audience's full attention is concentrated on the single dancer, so the dancer must perform with technical clarity and virtuosity. The solo performance is usually awarded to the most technically advanced dancer or one who exhibits a unique and exciting stage personality.

A group dance presents more possibilities in terms of floor pattern, spatial design, and movement interchange between dancers. As a result, fewer technical dance movements are needed for a successful piece of dance choreography.

In a group dance, all dancers need not be on the stage at the same time. Interesting floor patterns and spatial designs can be created with entrances and exits. Another means of creating interest is to vary the tempo, direction, or quality of a movement phrase as it is performed by different subgroups.

A group dance can also be diversified by solos, duets, trios, or quartets. A common choreography tool utilized in group dances is the *canon*; a canon is a round, such as "Three Blind Mice," in which the group is divided into subgroups that repeat and interact with one another. The effect of the canon is that each subgroup appears to be performing different movement phrases when, in fact, each subgroup is performing the same movement phrases, but at different times.

During the student's initial attempts at choreography, it is beneficial to experiment with both solo and group choreography. Choreography is a valuable experience, as it encourages creativity and discipline, thus promoting the overall development of the dance student.

JAZZ DANCE PERFORMANCE

Students in a jazz dance class may be given the opportunity to perform in a dance program. For some students, performance will be the highlight of the course, whereas other students may prefer not to be onstage. Students who do not wish to perform can learn a great deal by participating in the production aspects of the dance program.

Behind the Performance Scene

Listed below are jobs for the nonperforming dancer.

1. *Publicity*
   Advertisement design and distribution
   Program design and distribution
2. *Technical crew*
   Sound
   Lighting
   Costume design and wardrobe assistants
   Props and stagehands
   Makeup
   Ushering
3. *Organizing the dance program*
   The performance space
   The dance program
   The performance

This list may vary, depending upon the formality and size of the performance.

Advertisement Design and Distribution

Advertisements should include: title of the concert, performance group, place, date, time, fee, and a telephone number for further information. The design of the advertisement should be clear and easy to read, with a small graphic to attract attention. Advertisements should be posted locally and mailed to other dance studios, high schools, and colleges in the vicinity. School and local newspapers should be notified of details regarding the performance. All publicity should be distributed at least three weeks prior to the opening of the performance.

If it is a school performance, school facilities can help the performance budget. Flyers can be made using the school's duplicating machine. Large poster advertisements may be made in the school's art department. The art department may be willing to make advertisement design part of a class assignment.

Program Design and Distribution

The design of the program cover may be the same graphic as used for advertisements. The program contents should be typed, listing the order of the dances, musical selections, choreographer, and names of dancers appearing in each dance. The production crew should be given credit either at the beginning or end of the program contents. Programs should be made available prior to the concert and may be distributed by the usher.

Sound

Since the music is of utmost importance, a good sound system should be used. In most dance programs, the recording of the sound is done by a single person, whether it be the instructor, a member of the school audiovisual department, or a student with qualified technical skills. Recording the entire concert on one cassette tape or reel-to-reel recorder is necessary for smooth transitions. Allow short intervals between the selections, record at a consistent volume, and use new records if possible.

Lighting

Lighting for the dance performance may be done by students who are supervised by a person knowledgeable in lighting technique. Someone may be needed in the lighting booth to call cues for lighting, carry out the lighting commands, and run the spotlight. Students who participate in this area of technical operations may also be involved with theater productions or may be nondancers interested in developing this skill.

Costume Design and Wardrobe Assistants

In an informal concert, there may be minimal or no money budgeted for costuming. If costumes are needed, ingenuity will make something of nothing. Costumes should be kept simple, because changing space and time between dance numbers will be limited.

For costuming group dances, inexpensive ma-

terial can be used for scarves, sashes, vests, or wrap-around skirts. Old ties can add color and uniformity to the dance group. Brightly colored leotards with matching tights serve as good costumes. Dark leotards with brightly colored accessories can also be used. For solos and duets, the costumes list is endless—just visit a secondhand clothing store, and a wardrobe can be inexpensively designed. One or more students may be in charge of designing costumes. A student or groups of students may assist in the sewing of costumes, serve as wardrobe mistresses, or assist dancers with quick costume changes.

Props and Stagehands

Some dances may require the use of props and or sets. The requisition or making of a prop or set may be assigned to a student. It becomes the duty of the prop manager or an assigned stagehand to place the set or prop in the correct stage place or be responsible for giving each dancer the prop or props they may need for a specific dance. The stagehand is also responsible for collecting the prop at the end of the dance.

Makeup

The job of the makeup crew may be a fascinating experience for the nondancing student who wants to be involved with dance theater production. The makeup artist is a true artist indeed, working with a wide range of colors to make the face of the dancer become an integral part of the dancer's performance. Although for most dances the choreographer will probably request basic stage makeup, sometimes dance themes may lend themselves to elaborate makeup jobs. For even more special effects, body makeup may also be used to restate a dance theme.

Ushering

The job of the usher is to direct the audience to their seats and to hand out the dance programs. Ushers should arrive at the theater one hour before the start of the performance and should stand at the head of the aisles or at the entrance to the theater. A dressed-up appearance is appropriate for the usher.

The Performance Space

The dance studio can serve as the performance space for an informal dance concert. A backdrop may be needed to cover the mirror, *barres*, stereo equipment, etc. A few basic theater lights can be used to highlight the performance area and create a theatrical setting. Chairs with risers would provide excellent seating, but chairs alone would be adequate.

If it is a school performance and the school has a theater, the concert could be presented in a more formal manner. The technical aspects of the production should be discussed with the person in charge of theater management.

The Dance Program

Selection of dance pieces for the program and the order of their presentation is an integral part of the dance concert. An informal studio concert may consist of class work and student choreography, with the class warm-up as the show opener. The warm-up should be choreographed with minimal repetitions of movements and should include interesting movement directions, tempo changes, and spatial patterns. The choreographed warm-up may serve as a way to utilize all dancers. It will require rehearsal so that spacing and musical cues can be set.

The order of the program should offer variety. Intersperse solo dances between group dance numbers. Vary the mood by alternating fast and percussive numbers with more lyrical dance pieces. Dances with clever costuming or props should be distributed throughout the program. Start and end the program with lively group numbers. The opening dance must immediately capture the attention of the audience. The ending number should be technically sound but highly energetic, for it is what the audience will remember the most.

The Performance

In addition to numerous rehearsals, at least one nonstop run-through, or dress rehearsal, with costumes, props, and lighting, should occur before the performance. Preferably this rehearsal should occur the day before the opening date of the concert.

On the day of the performance, it is the dancer's responsibility to arrive at the theater or studio at least one hour before the concert begins, checking in with the teacher or the person in charge. Before the performance, the teacher or a student dance captain may lead a group warm-up. If a group warm-up is not scheduled, it is the dancer's responsibility to warm up adequately.

It is normal theatrical procedure to begin a performance five minutes after the scheduled time. The technical crew, backstage crew, and all performers will be alerted prior to the curtain opening. Once the program begins, the continuity of the show should be maintained by minimizing the time between performance pieces. Dancers should be aware of the ongoing stage performance to avoid missing any entrance cues.

It is evident that there is much to be learned from the initial dance performance experience. As more theatrical experience is attained, the dancer will develop into a seasoned performer.

Addenda

Appendix A. Checklist for a More Successful Dance Class

1. Arrive at class ten to fifteen minutes early to give yourself a pre–warm-up, such as the one described in Chapter 7.
2. Do not eat a heavy meal prior to class. A piece of fruit, yogurt, dried fruit, or nuts are recommended preclass snacks.
3. Come to class in the appropriate dance attire.
4. Clear your mind of outside interference when you enter the classroom. Be prepared to fully concentrate on the lesson.
5. Find a space to stand where you can see and hear the teacher. Allow yourself plenty of room so you can move and stretch freely.
6. Be sensitive to any injuries you might have. Give special attention to the injured area during pre–warm-up exercises as well as in class activities. Do not overstretch or otherwise stress injured body parts.
7. If there is a review or repetition of combinations from class to class, mentally go over the steps before class so that you will be prepared to either perform the combination or receive further choreographic instruction.
8. Do not be afraid to ask questions if you are unclear or want to improve your understanding of a certain technique.
9. Do not compare yourself to others in the class. However, learn to improve your performance by watching and imitating the more skilled dancers in the class.
10. Be aware of the ability level of the class in which you enroll. Do not take a class that is beyond your level, as it can lead to frustration. On occasion, a more advanced class may be fun for a challenge.
11. Participate in dance class to improve your skill, knowledge, and aesthetic sense, and to have a good time!

HAPPY DANCING!

Appendix B.
A Future In Jazz Dance

There are various career opportunities in the dance world in addition to that of professional performer. Dance talents may also be turned to the professions of dance rehearsal director, choreographer, and teacher. All of these careers require time, energy, ambition, and the patience to endure the technical training necessary to achieve highly developed dance expertise.

Versatility is essential for the dancer. In preparation for any dance career, the dancer should be committed to spending a great deal of time in class study, not only to develop dance skills, but also to develop a variety of dance styles. Singing and acting lessons may also help the dancer in securing work in the theater.

PROFESSIONAL DANCER

Employment opportunities as a professional dancer include musical theater, film and television (including variety shows, award shows, special programs, and commercials), and nightclub acts. Initially the dancer must attend as many auditions as possible, including "cattle call" auditions, to gain recognition from choreographers and directors.

On entering the audition, the dancer will be expected to present a résumé and professional photographs. The résumé should include name, address, phone number, hair and eye color (age, height, and weight are optional), and a list of all previous dance work. The professional photographs should include an 8″ x 10″ black and white glossy of a head shot and an 8″ x 10″ black and white glossy of a dance shot, on the bottom of which are listed the dancer's name and union membership. Also included may be four smaller action photographs featuring the dancer's unique dance abilities or photographs of different personality moods, or characteristics, known as a personality composite.

In the warm-up room prior to the audition, it is advisable (and considered good dance etiquette) to find a small corner or side of the room to do warm-up and stretching exercises. Often the warm-up can become a competition between dancers to show off their flexibility, turns, or other dance moves. More-experienced dancers may try to use the warm-up to intimidate a dancer new to auditions. Remember the intent of the warm-up period: to prepare yourself physically and mentally for the audition.

Directors and choreographers are often influenced by first impressions. Appearance is a major factor of the first impression. It is important to look neat and clean. Wear dance clothing that flatters your best features and plays down your worst features. It is beneficial for women dancers to show off their legs. Hair should be pulled away from the face but not secured ballet style. Makeup should be heavy day or evening makeup but not stage makeup. To maintain a fresh appearance, bring a towel to wipe perspiration. Finally, absolutely do not chew gum—not even to walk in the door.

Dancers should be prepared with ballet, tap, jazz, character, and tennis shoes. Warm-ups, leg warmers, and sweaters may also be needed for rest periods during the audition.

Generally an audition call will be for union dancers. If all the dance positions are not selected from the union dancers, then the audition will be open to nonunion dancers. Once a union job is secured, the dancer must join the union associated with the job. Listed below are the various entertainment unions and their areas of professional concentrations.

American Federation of Television and Radio Artists (AFTRA): television and radio, including commercials.

American Guild of Variety Artists (AGVA): nightclub entertainment.

Equity: theater.

Screen Actors Guild (SAG): film, motion pictures, commercials.

Screen Extras Guild (SEG): This is a good union for dancers because extras are less expensive to hire. A dancer may secure a job more easily as an extra than as a dancer merely because of financial reasons on the part of the hiring agency.

While a dancer is concentrating on obtaining professional dance work, there are other nonprofessional opportunities available as well. A growing number of dance companies perform and tour jazz dance. There are also special presentations of choreographers' new works. Although many of these jobs are done for free or with little pay, they offer the beginning dance performer an opportunity to gain exposure and performance practice.

Finally, the aspiring dancer must have a standby job to cover living expenses while developing a professional career. The job should have flexible hours so that the dancer can attend auditions.

DANCE REHEARSAL DIRECTOR

When a dancer has secured a professional dance position, a great deal of rehearsal time is invested in learning the dances of the choreographer. However, the choreographer will not preside over all rehearsals. Many choreographers spend initial rehearsals in teaching the dances and then return at a later date to view the progress of the dancers and to make additions and corrections to the dances. During the rehearsals, the most proficient dancer or a dancer that has previously worked with the choreographer will conduct rehearsals. That dancer is designated as the dance captain or dance rehearsal director.

CHOREOGRAPHER

In most cases, a choreographer was once a professional dancer who left the performance spotlight, first to teach, then to become an assistant choreographer, and finally to become a choreographer. A choreographer usually begins a career by working for community theaters, dance companies, colleges, junior colleges, or high schools. At first, some work may be done for limited pay, for expenses, or for free. A choreographer's success depends upon the response of people in the production end of the entertainment world. Choreographers should become acquainted with directors, producers, theater owners and leaders of theater organizations, and department chairmen. These people should be invited to any concerts or theatrical work done by the choreographer.

Work in choreography may also be found with a touring dance clinic for teachers, students, and professional groups. Choreographers are paid a substantial fee for a two- or three-day presentation on choreography. Examples of such dance clinic groups are Dance Masters of America and Dance Caravan.

Other choreography jobs may be found at summer dance camps. Here the talents of choreographer, teacher, and dance rehearsal director must be combined in choreographing and directing dance routines for college and high school dance groups. The camp is generally a four-day clinic in which choreographers direct three dance numbers. In addition, they are expected to give lectures and demonstrations in makeup, auditioning, dance technique, and choreography. The culmination of the dance camp clinic is a competitive performance by the student dance groups, which are judged on choreography, dance technique and execution, appearance, projection, and esprit de corps.

DANCE TEACHER

Dance teaching is perhaps the most secure profession in the dancer's world. A jazz dance teacher may find employment on a full-time or part-time basis in private or professional dance studios, in educational settings, and in recreation departments. Students may range from children to adults, and abilities from novice to advanced.

Proficiency in dance technique is required for all teaching positions. At the public high school level, a dance teacher must have a secondary level teaching credential. At the junior college and college level, a dance teacher must have a master's degree. In some instances, a master's degree may be waived if a dancer has had extensive professional dance experience. Colleges and universities may encourage instructors to continue their education toward a doctorate (Ph.D.) and may expect them to contribute to dance research and publications.

Another teaching area the jazz dance instructor may wish to investigate is the increasingly popular fitness form of jazz dance. Jazz fitness classes are a combination of jazz dance movements, calisthenics, and aerobic exercises.

In any teaching situation, it is the personality, knowledge, and abilities of the teacher that sustain a class. An ability to analyze and clarify movement and technique is essential for good teaching. A clear understanding of the needs of a student must also be developed.

Although not all dancers may choose a professional career, dance in itself is a medium that gives much physical, mental, and emotional fulfillment at whatever level it is pursued.

Appendix C.
Jazz Dance Music

Music is an essential ingredient of any jazz dance class and very often provides the motivation and focus necessary to maintain a high energy level. Music is generally used as an accompaniment to warm-up exercises and movement combinations and, at times, as a stimulus to improvisation and composition. Both live and recorded music can serve this purpose; however, recorded music, because of the wide variety of good jazz and popular music available, is most commonly used.

Music for the jazz dance class can be selected from many categories of jazz and popular music. Jazz can be strictly instrumental or contain vocal arrangements. It can vary from lyrical to funky or percussive. It can be free-form or metered. Jazz can also be categorized by its era: ragtime, swing, Dixieland, or bebop.

The versatility of jazz dance makes it adaptable to many styles of music other than strictly jazz. Good records for the jazz dance class can be found in record store collections under the categories of jazz, rock, soul, disco, new wave, reggae, blues, vocals, and show tunes. The following list provides some musical suggestions, with recommendations for their use in a jazz dance class. The list attempts to classify the artists into the sections in which they would be found in a record store.

JAZZ

The jazz music artists listed below are divided into seven categories. Each area of jazz retains a specific style that calls for this division. One aspect that is common to all these jazz forms, however, is the use of syncopation.

Metered Jazz

Metered jazz has an extremely obvious beat and is appropriate for warm-ups and combination work, as well as for choreography.

George Benson	L.A. Four
Dave Brubeck	Hubert Laws
Stanley Clark	Ramsey Lewis
The Crusaders	Chuck Mangione
Bill Evans	Herbie Mann
Chico Hamilton	Noel Pointer
Herbie Hancock	David Sanborn
Bob James	Tom Scott
Quincy Jones	Spyrogyra
John Klemmer	Tim Weisberg
Earl Klugh	

Free-form Jazz

Free-form jazz has no set meter. Because the meter changes throughout the music, the beat is less obvious than that of metered jazz. The artists listed below play mainly free-form jazz. Their recordings would be most appropriate for choreography and improvisation.

Anthony Braxton	Keith Jarrett
John Coltrane	Jean Luc Ponty
Chick Corea	Pharaoh Saunders
Miles Davis	Weather Report

Vocal Jazz

Vocal jazz is mainly metered, with occasional free-form sections. It is lots of fun, with nice energy and quality change, and is appropriate for combinations and choreography.

Manhattan Transfer	Lambert, Hendricks & Ross
Al Jarreau	

Swing/Big Band/Nostalgia

This music dates from the swing era of the thirties and forties. It is rhythmic, extremely stylistic, and is appropriate for combinations and choreography that reflect the swing style.

Count Basie	Earl Hines
Tommy Dorsey	Glenn Miller
Duke Ellington	Django Reinhardt
Benny Goodman	Artie Shaw
Woody Herman	

Ragtime

Ragtime dates from the late 1890s through the early 1900s. It is characterized by a syncopated beat in the melody. Ragtime is very metered and rhythmic and is fun for warm-ups, combinations, and choreography.

Eubie Blake
Scott Joplin

New Orleans Jazz

New Orleans jazz is characterized by a fast syncopated beat. It is fun to introduce in class for a specific combination.

Pete Fountain
Al Hirt

Latin Jazz

Latin jazz uses unusual percussion instruments. It is mainly metered and is excellent for warm-ups and combination work.

Herb Alpert	Ralph McDonald
Gato Barbieri	Cal Tjader

ROCK

Rock is popular music that combines the elements of rhythm and blues with country and western music and has a heavily accented beat. In all categories of rock, the beat is obvious and all-important.

Soul

Soul has its roots in gospel music. It has a blues quality with an upbeat tempo and is extremely danceable. It is excellent for warm-ups, locomotor movements, and combinations.

Aretha Franklin	Patti LaBelle
Four Tops	The Pointer Sisters
Isaac Hayes	Diana Ross
Isley Brothers	Sly and the Family Stone
Gladys Knight and the Pips	Temptations
	Stevie Wonder

Disco

Disco is an offshoot of soul, with influences from Latin music. It is extremely rhythmic and is usually in 4/4 meter. It is excellent for warm-ups, locomotor movements, and combinations. Some selections may be too repetitious for choreography.

Ashford and Simpson	Kool and the Gang
Chic	Lipps, Inc.
Linda Clifford	Stephanie Mills
Earth, Wind and Fire	Peaches and Herb
Gloria Gaynor	S.O.S. Band
Michael Jackson	Donna Summer

Hard Rock

Hard rock is rhythmic music with heavy metal instrumentation. It is metered music that is good for choreography as well as for class work.

Pat Benatar	Santana
The Commodores	Steely Dan
Doobie Brothers	Tower of Power
Teddy Pendergrass	Traffic

New Wave

New wave music is very repetitive and hypnotic in its presentation. It reminds one of the repetition used in primitive African music. It is mostly metered, although some of the recordings are free-form and conducive to relaxation.

Elvis Costello	Gary Numan
Brian Eno	The Pretenders
Grace Jones	The Talking Heads

Reggae

Reggae comes from Jamaica and is a mixture of Latin and soul in its sound. It is upbeat and filled with percussion instruments. Reggae music has an interesting syncopation that is fun to work with in combinations. Do experiment with it because it is extremely danceable.

Jimmy Cliff	Third World
Bob Marley	

BLUES

Blues is a musical form inherited from black musicians. It is usually slow in tempo and heavy in intensity and soul. It has a specific twelve-bar chordal sequence that rarely varies.

B.B. King	John Mayall
Taj Mahal	Johnny Guitar Watson

VOCALS

These vocal artists present strong dynamic changes in their songs and provide music that is good for light-hearted choreography as well as combination work.

Neil Diamond	Frank Sinatra
Bette Midler	Barbra Streisand
Liza Minnelli	

SHOW TUNES

Show tunes are usually choreographed numbers, so why not try a song from a favorite show for classroom choreography. New musicals keep appearing, so keep in touch with the latest.

A Chorus Line	*Godspell*
Ain't Misbehavin'	*Grease*
Annie	*Hair*
Fame	*West Side Story*
42nd Street	*The Wiz*

Appendix D.
Jazz Dance Films

Dance films are excellent for relating the history of dance art, its changing styles and techniques, as well as for presenting great performers and performances. The student can benefit from observing such films, not only for their historical information and technical value, but also for the inspiration they can provide. Although nothing is as powerful as a live performance, sometimes economics or the inaccessibility of live performances may make first-hand experience impossible. Dance films can be an exciting alternative.

A limited number of jazz dance films are available for a small rental fee through universities and public libraries. However, television can provide a full range of dance programming, including dance concerts, musical theater performances, and variety and nightclub acts. In addition, the nostalgic movies of the thirties, forties, and fifties feature such dance greats as Fred Astaire, Ginger Rogers, Gene Kelly, and many others.

INSTRUCTIONAL FILMS

Instructional films for jazz dance are limited. The ones listed below are excellent for increasing the students' awareness of jazz dance. They can be rented for a low to moderate fee from the distributors listed. They can also be rented from university multimedia departments across the country. Public libraries are another possible source for film rental.

Alvin Ailey: Memories and Versions
Presents selections ranging from blues to classical and opera.
54 minutes/16 mm/color/distributed by Phoenix, University of Illinois, and WNET.

America on Stage
Panoramic look at history of performing arts.
10 minutes/16 mm/distributed by MTP.

Echoes of Jazz
Traces development of American jazz dance from tap through orchestrated jazz of the 1930s and stylized theatrical form in the 1960s.
30 minutes/black and white/distributed by WNET New York, Northern Illinois University, Indiana University, Boston University, University of Minnesota, University of North Carolina, and Pennsylvania State University.

The Great Astaire
Features the talents of Fred Astaire, Paulette Goddard, and Artie Shaw and his orchestra. Includes an excerpt of feature film.
8 minutes/black and white/distributed by MGM and University of South Florida.

Lindy, Single Rhythm
Demonstrates a new technique for teaching the fascinating lindy. Shows a couple dancing through all ten lessons.
8 minutes/16 mm/black and white/distributed by Brigham Young University.

A Portrait of Contemporary Jazz Dance
Investigates rudiments, techniques, and style of jazz dance. Documents rehearsals and warm-up sessions and climaxes in a performance of "Angles of Impact" by the Jazz Dance Theater at Pennsylvania State University.
20 minutes/16 mm/distributed by Stoiac.

Sue's Leg: Remembering the 30s
Twyla Tharp and Company dance to the music of the late Fats Waller.
Part 1, 30 minutes/Part 2, 30 minutes/16 mm/distributed by IU and University of Illinois.

Tap Dancin'
Explores art of American tap dance through stage performances, candid interviews, and vintage film clips. Included are John Bubbles, Nicholas Brothers, Chuck Green, Honi Coles, Jazz Tap Ensemble, and Third Generation Step.
58 minutes/16 mm or video cassette/distributed by Blackwood Productions, Inc.

COMMERCIAL FILMS

The following commercial films are not available through university or film rental libraries, but many of them are shown frequently on television. The production company of each film is given for further information. The films are listed in chronological order and are valuable for examples of popular dances of the times, as well as for performances by dance greats.

Our Dancing Daughter
Joan Crawford does the Charleston.
MGM/1928.

After Seben
James Barton performs a solo eccentric dance. Three pairs of lindy dancers from the Savoy Ballroom, including George "Shorty" Snowden, perform the early lindy. Steps include examples of the Charleston, breakaway, and cakewalk. Music furnished by the Chick Webb Orchestra.
Paramount/1929.

The Gay Divorcee
Fred Astaire and Ginger Rogers.
RKO Radio/1934.

The Little Colonel
Bill Robinson and Shirley Temple.
Fox Film Corp./1935.

The Littlest Rebel
Bill Robinson and Shirley Temple.
20th Century–Fox/1935.

Roberta
Fred Astaire and Ginger Rogers.
RKO Radio/1935.

Top Hat
Fred Astaire and Ginger Rogers.
RKO Radio/1935.

San Francisco
Cakewalk production number.
MGM/1936.

Swing Time
Fred Astaire and Ginger Rogers.
RKO Radio/1936.

Damsel in Distress
Fred Astaire.
RKO Radio/1937.

How to Dance the Shag
Arthur Murray instructional film.
Skibo Productions, Inc./1937.

Shall We Dance?
Fred Astaire and Ginger Rogers.
RKO Radio/1937.

Carefree
Fred Astaire and Ginger Rogers.
RKO Radio/1938.

Everybody Sing
Whitey's Lindy Hoppers.
MGM/1938.

Just Around the Corner
Bill Robinson and Shirley Temple.
20th Century–Fox/1938.

The Story of Vernon and Irene Castle
Fred Astaire and Ginger Rogers.
RKO Radio/1939.

Hellzapoppin'
Lindy Hop Dancers.
Universal/1941.

Star-Spangled Rhythm
Katherine Dunham.
Paramount/1942.

Du Barry Was a Lady
Gene Kelly.
MGM/1943.

Stormy Weather
Bill Robinson, the Nicholas Brothers, and Katherine Dunham.
20th Century–Fox/1943.

Cavalcade of Dance
Veloz and Yolanda review of the dance craze.
Warner Bros./1944.

Anchors Aweigh
Gene Kelly.
MGM/1945.

Ziegfeld Follies
Fred Astaire.
MGM/1946.

The Pirate
Gene Kelly and the Nicholas Brothers.
MGM/1948.

The Barkleys of Broadway
Fred Astaire and Ginger Rogers.
MGM/1949.

On the Town
Gene Kelly and Ann Miller.
MGM/1949.

Yes Sir, That's My Baby
Donald O'Connor.
Universal-International/1949.

An American in Paris
Gene Kelly.
MGM/1951.

Royal Wedding
Fred Astaire.
MGM/1951.

The Belle of New York
Fred Astaire.
MGM/1952.

Singin' in the Rain
Gene Kelly and Donald O'Connor.
MGM/1952.

Brigadoon
Gene Kelly.
MGM/1954.

Daddy Long Legs
Fred Astaire.
20th Century–Fox/1955.

Silk Stockings
Fred Astaire.
MGM/1957.

Dance Beat
Rod Alexander discusses dance as based on rhythm, beginning with early ritual dance.
20th Century–Fox/1958.

Hey, Let's Twist
Peppermint Loungers.
Paramount/1961.

Twist Around the Clock
Chubby Checker.
Columbia/1961.

Bibliography

CHAPTER 1: JAZZ DANCE: A HISTORY

Ellfeldt, Lois. *Dance: From Magic to Art*. Dubuque, Iowa: William C. Brown, 1976.

Emery, Lynne Fauley. *Black Dance in the United States from 1619 to 1970*. Palo Alto, Calif.: Mayfield, 1972.

Giordano, Gus. *Anthology of American Jazz Dance*. Evanston, Ill.: Orion, 1978.

Kelly, Kelvin. "Tony, Emmy, Oscar, and Bob," in Broadway show program of *Dancin'*, 1978.

Luigi, and Wydro, Kenneth. *The Luigi Jazz Dance Technique*. Garden City, N.Y.: Doubleday, 1981.

Missett, Judi Sheppard. *Jazzercise*. New York: Bantam Books, 1978.

Sabatine, Jean. *Technique and Styles of Jazz Dancing*. Waldwick, N. J.: Hoctor Dance Records, 1969.

Stearns, Marshall, and Stearns, Jean. *Jazz Dance: The Story of American Vernacular Dance*. New York: Schirmer Books, 1964.

CHAPTER 2: GETTING STARTED

Hammond, Sandra Noll. *Ballet Basics*. Palo Alto, Calif.: Mayfield, 1974.

Penrod, James, and Plastino, Janice Gudde. *The Dancer Prepares: Modern Dance for Beginners*. Palo Alto, Calif.: Mayfield, 1980.

CHAPTER 3: A DANCER'S POSTURE

Drury, Blanche. *Posture and Figure Control Through Physical Education.* Palo Alto, Calif.: National Press Publishing, 1970.

Rathbone, Josephine, and Hunt, Valerie. *Corrective Physical Education.* Philadelphia: Saunders, 1965.

Sweigard, Lulu E. *Human Movement Potential.* New York: Dodd, Mead, 1974.

Todd, Mabel. *The Thinking Body.* New York: Dance Horizons, 1937.

Wells, Katherine F. *Kinesiology.* Philadelphia: Saunders, 1971.

CHAPTER 4: BALLET FOR THE JAZZ DANCER

Hammond, Sandra Noll. *Ballet Basics.* Palo Alto, Calif.: Mayfield, 1974.

Hammond, Sandra Noll. *Ballet: Beyond the Basics.* Palo Alto, Calif.: Mayfield, 1982.

Kirstein, Lincoln; Stuart, Muriel; and Dyer, Carlus. *The Classic Ballet: Basic Technique and Terminology.* New York: Knopf, 1977.

Shook, Karel. *Elements of Classical Ballet Technique.* New York: Dance Horizons, 1977.

Vaganova, Agrippina. *Basic Principles of Classical Ballet.* New York: Dover, 1969.

CHAPTER 5: BASIC JAZZ DANCE

Giordano, Gus. *Anthology of American Jazz Dance.* Evanston, Ill.: Orion, 1978.

Hutchinson, Ann. *Labanotation.* New York: Dance Notation Bureau, 1970.

Kinkead, Mary Ann. *Elementary Labanotation.* Palo Alto, Calif.: Mayfield, 1982.

Sabatine, Jean. *Technique and Styles of Jazz Dancing.* Waldwick, N. J.: Hoctor Dance Records, 1969.

CHAPTER 6: PUTTING IT ALL TOGETHER

Ammer, Christine. *Harper's Dictionary of Music.* New York: Harper & Row, 1972.

Dimondstein, Geraldine. *Children Dance in the Classroom.* New York: Macmillan, 1971.

Hayes, Elizabeth. *Dance Composition and Production.* New York: Ronald Press, 1955.

Lockhart, Aileene. *Modern Dance.* Dubuque, Iowa: William C. Brown, 1966.

Murray, Ruth. *Dance in Elementary Education.* New York: Harper & Row, 1953.

Sherbon, Elizabeth. *On the Count of One: Modern Dance Methods,* 3rd ed. Palo Alto, Calif.: Mayfield, 1982.

CHAPTER 7: THE DANCER'S INSTRUMENT: TAKING CARE OF IT

Allsen, Phillip E.; Harrison, Joyce M.; and Vance, Barbara. *Fitness for Life: An Individualized Approach.* Dubuque, Iowa: William C. Brown, 1975.

Benjamin, Ben E. *Sports Without Pain.* New York: Summit Books, 1979.

Bogert, L. Jean; Briggs, George M.; and Calloway, Doris Howes. *Nutrition and Physical Fitness.* Philadelphia: Saunders, 1966.

Davis, Adelle. *Let's Eat Right to Keep Fit.* Harcourt, Brace & World, 1954.

Featherstone, Donald F. *Dancing Without Danger.* Cranbury, N. J.: A. S. Barnes, 1970.

Klafs, Carl E., and Arnheim, Daniel D. *Modern Principles of Athletic Training.* St. Louis: C. V. Mosby, 1969.

Miller, David K., and Allen, T. Earl. *Fitness: A Lifetime Commitment.* Minneapolis: Burgess, 1979.

Mott, Jane A. *Conditioning and Basic Movement Concepts.* Dubuque, Iowa: William C. Brown, 1968.

APPENDIX C: JAZZ DANCE MUSIC

Cayou, Dolores. *Modern Jazz Dance.* Palo Alto, Calif.: Mayfield, 1971.

APPENDIX D: JAZZ DANCE FILMS

Stearns, Marshall, and Stearns, Jean. *Jazz Dance: The Story of American Vernacular Dance.* New York: Schirmer Books, 1964.

Family of Characters: Minda Goodman Kraines, Ruth Cavagnaro, Sue Berge, Niccola Moore, Young Kim, Floyd Bigornia, Pat Howard, and Robin Bellerive.

Index

accent, 73
African dance, 3–4, 8
Afro-Haitian dance, 9
Afro jazz, 90
Ailey, Alvin, 10, 103
alignment, 26–27, 30–33
All That Jazz, 16
American Bandstand, 11
An American in Paris, 11
Anthology of American Jazz Dance, 14
appearance, 20, 97
arabesque, 41
arch, 46
arms, ballet positions of, 37–38
Armstrong, Louis, 3, 7
assemblé, 68
Astaire, Fred, 8, 9, 103–106
attitude, 41
auditions, 96–97

Baker, Josephine, 6
ballet
    and jazz dance, 9, 90
    principles of movement in, 42–43
    technique, 35–43
barre, 21
Basie, Count, 7
battement dégagé, 40
battement tendu, 40
beat, 72
Beatles, 13, 73
Beatty, Talley, 10
Bells Are Ringing, 15
Bennett, Michael, 15
Bernstein, Leonard, 11
big apple, 6
big bands, 7
black bottom, 6, 11
black choreographers, 10

black dancers, 4–5, 6, 10
blues, 6, 7, 11, 101
body care, 81–87
body roll, 50
body wave, 50
Bojangles. *See* Robinson, Bill "Bojangles"
boogie woogie, 8
breakaway, 8, 104
breathing, 33
Broadway, 7, 9, 11, 15–16, 17
Brubeck, Dave, 73
buck and wing, 4
Bujones, Fernando, 10
bump, 15
bus stop, 15

Cabaret, 16
cakewalk, 4, 5, 6, 104
careers, dance, 96–98
Castle, Vernon and Irene, 6
Castle walk, 6
chaîne turn, 65
Champion, Gower, 3, 11
Charleston, 6, 11, 104, 105
chassé, 57, 64
Chicago, 15
chicken, 11
choreography, jazz dance, 14, 91, 98
A Chorus Line, 15, 88–89
class, jazz dance, 21–22, 95
clinics, dance, 98
clog, English, 4
clothing, 20
Cole, Jack, 3, 9
collapse, 77
combinations, dance, 22, 78–79
contraction, 46
cramps, 85

Damn Yankees, 15
Dance Caravan, 98
Dance Masters of America, 98
Dancin', 16, 24–25, 80
Dean Martin–Jerry Lewis Show, 14
de Mille, Agnes, 9
demi-plié, 39
Depression, 7
diagonal flat back, 47
dimension, 76
direction, 75, 76
disco, 101
discos, 15
discotheques, 13, 15
Dixieland, 6, 7
Dorsey, Jimmy, 7
Dorsey, Tommy, 7
downbeat, 73
Dunham, Katherine, 10, 11, 90, 105
dynamics, 71, 76–77

East Indian dance, 13
Ed Sullivan Show, 14
education, dance, 98
Ellington, Duke, 7
etiquette, 21
Evans, Bill, 73

Facciuto, Eugene Louis (Luigi), 14
Fancy Free, 9, 10
fan kick, 63
feet, ballet positions of, 36
films, dance, 103–106
first aid, 84–86
flat back, 46
Forty-second Street, 3
Fosse, Bob, 15–16
fox trot, 6

frug, 13
funky/disco jazz, 90

Gennaro, Peter, 11
Giordano, Gus, 14, 15
Goodman, Benny, 7
gospel music, 11
grand battement, 41
grand plié, 39

hillbilly music, 11
hinge, 47
history, jazz dance, 3–17, 104
hitchhiker, 13
hitch kick, 60–63
hop, 68
Hullabaloo, 14
hustle, 15

ice, 84–85
improvisation
    as African dance style, 4
    and breakaway, 8
    and jazz dance, 45
    and jitterbug, 8
    and lindy hop, 8
    and rock, 13
    and swing, 7
injuries, 84–86
isolation movements, 22, 55–56
    and Jack Cole, 9
    and Gus Giordano, 14
    and Matt Mattox, 12–13
    and warmup, 21

Jazz Dance Chicago, 15, 18–19, 34
jazz dance styles, 90
jazz music
    Dixieland, 6, 7

history of, 4–17
and jazz dance, 4–17
Latin, 100
lyrical, 90
modern, 9
origins of, 4
selections of, for jazz dance, 99–100
symphonic, 7
jazz slide, 60
jazz split, 47, 53
jazz square, 60
jazz walks, 57
Jazz with Luigi, 14
jerk, 13
jeté, 69
jig, Irish, 4, 7
jitterbug, 8, 11
Joffrey Ballet, 5
jumps, 43, 67–69

Kelly, Gene, 9, 11, 103, 105, 106
kick-ball change, 64
kicks, 60–64
Kidd, Michael, 11
Kismet, 9

lateral, 48
Latin dance, 9
Latin jazz, 100
Laugh-In, 14
leap, 69
level, 75–76
lindy, 11, 104, 105
lindy hop, 8
Little Me, 15–16
Liza with a Z, 16
locomotor movements, 22, 57–69
Luigi. *See* Facciuto, Eugene Louis
lunge, 48

Man of La Mancha, 9
marathons, dance, 7
mashed potato, 11
Mattox, Matt, 12–13
measure, 72
meter, 72, 73
Miller, Glenn, 7
minstrel shows, 4–6
modern dance, 9
monkey, 13
muscle soreness, 84
music. *See* jazz music
music, jazz dance, 99–102
musical comedy, 5, 6, 7, 9
musical phrase, 74

New Girl in Town, 15
new wave music, 17, 101
Nicks, Walter, 10
note values, 72, 73
nutrition, 86–87

offbeat, 11
Oklahoma, 9
On the Town, 9
oppositional moves, 64
origins of jazz dance, 3–4

paddle turn, 65
Pajama Game, 15
pas de bourrée, 57–59
passé, 42
percussive movement, 76
performance, jazz dance, 92–94
Perry Como Show, 14
pimp's walk, 11
Pippin, 16
piqué turn, 66
pirouette, 66
pivot turn, 65

placement, 27–29, 30–33
plié, 39
pogo, 17
positions
    arm, 37–38
    foot, 36
    jazz dance, 45–48
postural muscles, 26
posture, 25–33
Presley, Elvis, 11, 13
Primus, Pearl, 10
projection, 71–72, 77–78
punk rock, 17

Radio City Music Hall, 71
ragtime, 5, 6, 7, 100
Redhead, 15
rehearsal director, 97
Reinking, Ann, 80
relevé, 40
"Requiem for a Slave," 14
rest, 73
résumés, 96
rhythm
    African, 4
    jazz, 4
    modern jazz, 9
    swing, 4
    syncopated. *See* syncopation
rhythmic pattern, 73–74
Robbins, Jerome, 9, 11
Robinson, Bill "Bojangles," 6–7, 104, 105
rock 'n' roll, 11, 101
Rogers, Ginger, 9, 103, 104, 105
roller coaster, 15
Runnin' Wild, 6

Savoy Ballroom, 7
Say Darling, 13
shag, 105

Shaw, Artie, 7
shimmy, 13
Shindig, 14
shin splints, 85–86
Shuffle Along, 6
sissonne, 68
slam dancing, 17
social dancing, 4, 9, 13
soft shoe, 4
solo dancing, 4, 8, 93
soul music, 101
soutenu turn, 67
space, 71, 75–76
spatial pattern, 75, 76
spotting, 43
sprain, 85
stage directions, 75
stag leap, 69
strain, 85
stretches, 48–56
studios, dance, 13
suspension, 77
sustained movement, 76
Sweet Charity, 16
swim, 13
swing (movement), 77
swing (music), 7, 100, 105
syncopation
  and buck and wing, 4
  defined, 5, 73
  and jazz dance, 5
  and jazz music, 5
  and lindy hop, 8
  and ragtime, 5, 100

rhythmic pattern of, 74
and symphonic jazz, 7

tabletop position, 46
tap dance, 7, 104
teaching, jazz dance, 98
technique, jazz dance, 9, 14
television, and jazz dance, 11, 13, 14, 16, 17
tempo, 72
Tharp, Twyla, 104
time, 71, 72–75
time signature, 72
training, jazz dance, 90
triplet, 59
turnout, 36, 38
turns, 43, 64–67
twist, 13, 106

unions, 97
upbeat, 73

vibratory movement, 76–77

Waller, Fats, 104
warmup, 21, 48–56, 81–84
West Indian dance, 9
West Side Story, 11
Whiteman, Paul, 7
Williamson, Liz, 44
World War I, 6
World War II, 9

yoga, 14

Other Mayfield books for dancers:

The Dancer Prepares: Modern Dance for Beginners, 2nd Edition

By James Penrod and Janice Gudde Plastino

This inexpensive text is a practical and thorough overview of modern dance written for male and female beginning dancers. Information is given on basic positioning and technique. In addition, there are valuable hints on the care of the body and a brief history of modern dance.

On the Count of One: Modern Dance Methods, 3rd Edition

By Elizabeth Sherbon

This revised edition of the popular intermediate-level modern dance text provides a base for sound technical training plus excellent guidelines for the future dance teacher. Labanotation has been added to most illustrated exercises, and there is enough material for two years of lesson plans.

57-60
71-79 +
TERMINOLOGY

p.36